GOD. GIFTS. YOU.
A Six-Week Study

Your Unique Calling and Design

Shirley Giles Davis

Dedication

To Maggie for teaching and showing me what Discernment looks like in so many meaningful and challenging ways.

To Nancy for demonstrating Mercy and courage every day and always. I have learned much of what mercy is by doing life together with you.

To Debby—your gift of Knowledge is constantly present and always helpful. I count on you for that.

To Grace and Allie who inspire me daily as you faithfully and avidly pursue your callings. I am in awe of your approach to obstacles not as limitations but simply as challenges to be overcome.

Thank you to each of you for listening to God's voice and living into your unique calling and design.

Acknowledgements

I am indebted to the Rev. Gwen Brown who asked me to serve on an early iteration of the Lay Ministries Team at First Pres Boulder, and to that team (Shelley, Kris, Alan, Gwen, Diana, Beth, Sally, and Monica) who lived such a fabulous example of the Body of Christ. Each person brought unique gifts and passion and skills to that Dream Team! Such a moment in time—God clearly working in and through us.

I am grateful to the Rev. Don Meeks who asked me to become the Director of EquipConnectServe Ministries—and who refused to accept my "no" for an answer. My six-month "I'll do this as a consultant and then you can hire the right person" has turned into over 19 amazing years at the church that is also my family and my home. Don's subsequent insistence on my creating the ECS Prayer Team before actually launching into projects was simultaneously the most frustrating and the wisest advice. The faithful prayers of that early team of seven (now over 50) invited God's power, presence, guidance, and activity into our equipping efforts—and I stand astounded at the obstacles God removed and the blessings He bestowed! The Lord continues to work powerfully through this dedicated team of prayer warriors.

I am thankful for a husband who was supportive of me doing this job in addition to my consulting. He was a great champion of me scaling back less essential committments to focus on equipping others in ministry and beyond.

My gratitude to the congregation of First Pres and numerous churches who have allowed me to help equip their congregations to serve is boundless. From my first tentative teaching on the context of love in the Body of Christ over 20 years ago to the writing of this book, equipping ministry has provided me a valuable learning laboratory and a front-row seat to what God is doing in and through His people.

Ultimately, God deserves the glory—for the call, for the equipping, for the gifting, for the correcting and training, for anything that may have resulted from EquipConnectServe Ministries. The Body of Christ is HIS idea. Spiritual Gifts are the tools of HIS plan. Call is part of how He empowers and scatters us into every arena, locally and globally.

Thanks to my current and former ECS Team members for your faithful, prayerful, insightful commitment and guidance all these years: Eric Erickson, Curt Hill, Willie Knierim, Jane Pampel, Ashley Matthews, Judy Pierce, Allan Harvey, Betsy Remnant, and Jen Koschmann.

Thank you to Lonni Pearce, Lynnie Parr, and Allan Harvey for your workbook editing expertise, and to Jane Pampel, Deb Gregory, and Judy Pierce for being "homework" guinea pigs. Many thanks to the assessment development team: Alan Brockett, Jen Koschmann, and Allan Harvey. Heartfelt gratitude goes to my multi-talented graphic designer, Ashley Matthews of Studio Anna Boulder. To the brilliant Alan Brockett who returned to the team to help us navigate the creation of the online inventory—there simply are no adequate words of praise!

Contents

Introduction

My heart's desire and my job for over twenty years (in fact, maybe part of my spiritual DNA from birth) has been to help individuals and churches figure out God's call, discover how they are gifted, see where and how they are motivated, and assist them in connecting all of that to every aspect of their lives.

Having taught and facilitated countless conversations and classes on spiritual gifts and call over the past twenty-five years, I've wished for a book like this one. This book is intended both as a study guide and a resource—for individuals, for small groups, for whole churches—seeking to go deeper in understanding and living out the Biblical mandate of being the Body of Christ.

Everything here is grounded in Scripture. God's Word is rich in both information and inspiration. Spend the time looking up the verses and saturating yourself in what God says about you, about gifts, about call, and about His desire for His church—His gathered and scattered people.

How to use these materials

This workbook is designed as a six-week study. Do it on your own or within the context of an existing or newly-created small group—where you'll have support, affirmation, accountability, and the collective wisdom of those gathered. Bring it to your church as a series for women, a men's study, a young adult or couples' course, a Sunday School class, or as a series for your whole congregation.

Every week is designed with daily homework. Plan to set aside 20-40 minutes each day to respond to the questions, reflect on what they mean to you, and converse with God. Weekly Small Group Discussion Guides are provided to help focus your conversation.

The first time you meet, be sure each participant has a *God. Gifts. You.* workbook, watch the "Calling" video and use the Discussion Guide on page 9.

Each week corresponds with a 20 minute video teaching for the following week. These sessions may be found at GodGiftsYou.com. Instructions and passwords for accessing these are provided on the video notes page for each week. If you prefer a DVD, that is also available at GodGiftsYou.com.

- Individually do the week's homework.
- Meet with your small group for discussion.
- Watch the video for the following week

Benefits of doing this study

This study will help you know more about your unique calling, the church as the Body of Christ, your own spiritual gifts, and how you might best serve Him in the church, your family, your workplace, the community, and the world.

Knowing your God-given call and giftedness can help you focus on meaningful, fulfilling service, while giving you the freedom and permission to say "no" to too many scattered life-draining commitments. You can gain clarity on your calling and experience the pleasure of God as you live into your gifts and know you are making an impact for eternity.

For churches that desire to see more meaningful engagement of their congregations, this study can be culture-altering. Working through the Scriptures, concepts and video teaching sessions in *God. Gifts. You.* may help elevate simple volunteering to fully-committed service. You may see people re-energized as they embrace their passions. As people use their newly-discovered gifts, they will feel more connected to what God is doing in and through them. And your church may experience greater unity as you explore the diversity of each person's unique design.

For those of you who already know your gifts and wonder if this book is worth your time, keep in mind that:
- Our calling(s) can change over time; our gifts may too.
- We need to continually be asking God throughout our lives how He wishes us to use our gifts.
- A key role for those who may be a step ahead in gift-understanding is to recognize, call out and affirm the gifts in others.
- We spend very little time talking about the universal call and individual call of God upon our churches and ourselves. This study helps re-emphasize those concepts.

An Adventure

God. Gifts. You. will take you on a journey to discover your own unique calling and design. You are tailor-made by a loving God. Come experience new freedom and bask in God's pleasure as you align yourself with how He has made you. Let's step into this adventure!

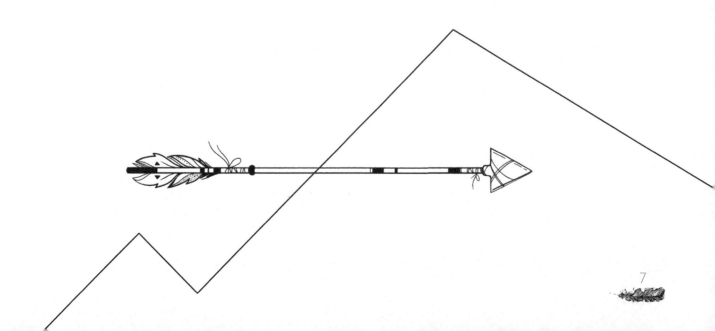

Intro to Week One: Discussion Guide

After watching the video, if you are in a large group setting, divide into groups of 5-6. Consider having these same groupings for the entire six weeks of the study.

Designate a facilitator for your small group – one who can help the group move through the questions and end on time.

Brief Introduction:
- What is your name?
- Where do you live?
- How long have you participated in these sorts of small group studies?

Once everyone has had a chance to share, ask each person to:
- Tell the group one thing about your vocation or how you spend your weekdays.
- Tell the group something about your family and/or your favorite hobby.

Finally, ask each person to share:
- What is one thing you hope to learn during these six weeks studying *God. Gifts. You.*?
- Encourage participants to jot their "one thing" down here:

Close your time together in prayer.

VIDEO NOTES

calling

Week One

calling

Dictionary.com defines "calling" as vocation, profession, or trade. It also has the meaning of a call or summons, a strong impulse or inclination, or even a convocation or bringing together of a group. "Call" can be a noun (as in the previous definitions) or a verb, meaning to cry out, to shout, to command, to ask to come, to invite, or even "to rouse from sleep, as by a call; waken."[1]

In each case, the sense is of an invitation or a summons *either away* from something or *to* something—often both simultaneously. There's also the sense of being specifically named or "called" as well as the implication of call being connected to a person's destiny.

In the Bible, the word "call" and its variations is used over 700 times (754 in the New International Version). These uses cover everything from The Creator naming day and night to the Lord calling individuals and peoples, to people calling out to God. Unfortunately, in most churches today, we hear very little preached or taught on how to discover, understand, and pursue our calling(s). If we do hear the term used, it is more often than not used to refer to someone in paid professional Christian ministry. This focus, while leaving out the vast majority of believers, also leaves us wondering if God speaks to us in the same way with the same importance. We are left struggling to make meaning out of our outside-of-church lives, instead of living fully into the fact that God has called you and me, individually and together, to be His people everywhere and in everything.

Let's take a look at some examples of God's call.

THIS WEEK'S STUDY GUIDES

DAY ONE: NAMES, AGES, STAGES, HEARING
DAY TWO: LISTENING, RECEPTIVITY, RESPONSE
DAY THREE: COMMISSIONING, ROLES, PLACEMENT
DAY FOUR: POSITION, PURPOSE, INFLUENCE
DAY FIVE: CALLING AND IMPACT
SMALL GROUP DISCUSSION GUIDE FOR WEEK ONE

DAY ONE   NAMES, AGES, STAGES, HEARING

The Call of Abram and Sarai

Read Genesis 12:1-9.

What does the Lord call Abram to do?

What does the Lord promise to do for Abram?

What is Abram's response to God's call to leave and go to a place God would show him?

How old was Abram at this time?
How old are you right now?

Do you believe that God can call you at any age, in any stage of your life? Why or why not?

What's your reaction to the Lord asking Abram to move away from his home and family?

What's your reaction to Abram not knowing his ultimate destination?

Who else was impacted by the Lord's call on Abram's life?

Do you see a time in your past or currently where God's call on your life has significantly impacted others (friends, family, co-workers, etc.)? Do you see a time when God's call on someone else's life has significantly impacted you? Briefly describe:

Look back at verses 7 and 8. Although Abram is not yet at his final destination, what does he choose to do in this place of limbo? (List at least two things.)

Part of the meaning of "calling" is "naming" or, sometimes, "re-naming." Through the course of Abram and Sarai's relationship with The Almighty God, He renames them. When God makes His covenant with Abram, God changes Abram's name to Abraham—from a name meaning "exalted father" to "father of a nation" (or "father of a multitude"). Sarai's name meant "princess." God changes her name to Sarah, meaning "princess—the mother of nations." (For more on this, read Genesis 17:1-22.)

Where is God renaming you? Has He renamed you as an adopted son or daughter through Christ? (Romans 8:14-17) Has He changed your name from father or mother to father or mother of nations—saying that you are blessed to be a blessing to many? From Simon the fisherman to Peter the one who fishes for people? From Saul the persecutor of the church to Paul the faithful Jesus-follower and church-planter? Jot your reflections here:

The Lord Calls the Prophet Samuel

Read 1 Samuel 3:1-11.
What happens in verses 4, 6, and 8?

In each case, Samuel's response is immediate. Write down his response:

What is the communication problem? (See verse 7.)

How does Eli help guide Samuel's understanding and response? (See verses 8-9.)

When Samuel realizes it is the Lord speaking, what is his response?

Where might you need help in discerning whether it is God's voice that you are hearing?

Who might be your "Eli"—someone who can listen with you?

This week, consider asking that person to help you discern God's voice in this season of your life.

Reflect

- Are you called to "leave and go" like Abraham and Sarah? Are you feeling the nudge to move to a new place (literally or symbolically)?
- Are you being called to be God's spokesperson like Samuel?

DAY TWO   LISTENING, RECEPTIVITY, RESPONSE

God Calls Moses

Read Exodus 3:1-10.
What was Moses doing and where was he when the angel of God appeared to him?

How ready or able are you to listen to God whenever, wherever? When you are going along doing your every-day things? During your work week?

In verse 4, what are God's first words to Moses? What is Moses' immediate response?

What is the problem that the Lord details?

According to verse 10, what will be Moses' role—Moses' call?

Moses seems to have a pattern of saving or rescue in his life from an early age—rescued from the Nile in a basket as an infant so he would grow up in Pharaoh's household; attempting to save a Hebrew slave by killing the Egyptian who was beating him; intervening to liberate the seven Midianite shepherdesses from marauding shepherds. His passion for deliverance finally comes together with God's call to free the Israelites from bond-age—late in life. Moses was then 80 years old.

Do you have a pattern in your life that might point to the theme of your calling? If yes, what is it?

Let's take a look at Moses' response(s) to God's command and summons:

Passage	God says	Moses says
Exodus 3:10-11		
Exodus 3:12-13		
Exodus 3:14 – 4:1		
Exodus 4:2-10		
Exodus 4:11-17		

Think about your own life. Where are you hearing God, but your excuses for delaying sound a lot like Moses—Who am I to do this? What if they do not believe me? I'm not up to the task you are asking me to do! Please send someone else!

REFLECT

Basically, all of Moses' responses boil down to one: "Lord, I'm afraid." In turn, all of the Lord's responses back to Moses boil down to one: "Trust Me—I AM able." Spend some time reviewing all the "God says" passages in the previous table. **PRAY THROUGH THEM** as an intercession to an Almighty Father who can and will make you able to do what He asks of you.

DAY THREE   COMMISSIONING, ROLES, PLACEMENT

*W*e have looked at Abram and Sarai following God's call into the unknown, knowing that their call was linked somehow to God's promise to expand their family and bless the nations of the world far beyond their generation. We reflected on Samuel, with the help of a mentor, learning to recognize and listen to God's voice. We looked at Moses whose life theme seems to have been freedom and rescue of the oppressed. We discovered that even when God is quite specific with His call, as He was to Moses, we may personally have lots of "thanks, but do not pick me for this assignment" responses.

In today's study, we continue in our exploration of calling—being named, spoken to, designed by and equipped by God to carry out His purposes and work in the world.

The Prophet Isaiah

Read Isaiah 6:1-8.
How does Isaiah receive his commission from the Lord?

In verse 5, what is Isaiah's response to seeing God in His glory?

Why are verses 5-7 important in Isaiah's preparation, readiness, and assurance?

Where might you need to confess your shortcomings, guilt, or sins—things that are separating you from God and from hearing Him or seeing Him more clearly?

TAKE SOME TIME NOW TO PRAY ABOUT THIS and ask the Lord to take away your guilt as you acknowledge that Jesus, once for all, has atoned for your guilt and your sin. End your prayer time by reading the reassurance found in 1 John 1:9: "If we confess our sins, He is faithful and just and will forgive us our sins and purify us from all unrighteousness."

What, then, is Isaiah's response to God seeking a spokesperson, a prophet who will go speak to His people?

Whatever the Lord asks you, how ready do you think you are to say "Here I am"?

0	**1**	**2**	**3**	**4**	**5**	**6**	**7**	**8**	**9**	**10**

Not at all ready   Ready no matter the cost

What is one area of your life, right now, that you ARE willing to say "Here I am! Send me"?

Take a moment to praise God for that clarity…or to pray for that kind of courage.

As we dig deeper into the concept of understanding call, you will notice many more scenarios in Scripture that are meant to encourage us to seek God and His call on our lives as individuals.

The Judge Deborah

Read Judges 4:1-5.
List four roles that Deborah plays:
1.
2.
3.
4.

Read Judges 5:6-7. Add a fifth role described of Deborah in verse 7.

Note in Judges 5:31b the result of Deborah's leadership:

In the table below, list some of the roles you currently fill. Then, go back and write in the impact you are having in those places. This can help you see where you are fulfilling a calling and where God is at work, especially, sometimes by hindsight.

Your Role	Impact

Jot down anything that came to mind as you completed that table relative to how God might be speaking to you right now:

The Captive Daniel

If you know the story of Daniel, you know that he was taken captive by King Nebuchadnezzar's troops after the siege of Jerusalem in 605 B. C. Daniel was removed from his home and brought to Babylon. He and other royals like him were to be trained and educated for three years so that they might serve in the king's palace. (For more on this, read Daniel 1:1-20.)

You are likely not a prisoner of war like Daniel and his friends. However, you may feel like you are working or serving in a place that is hostile to your faith and/or a context that feels uncomfortable for a variety of reasons. Take encouragement from Daniel's story as God equips him.

Read Daniel 1:9. What is the advantage given to Daniel by God?

Additionally, what gift or character trait(s) do you think Daniel exhibits in Daniel 1:11-16?

And, with what else did God equip Daniel and his friends? (See Daniel 1:17.)

Read Daniel 1:18-20. How does God's equipping position this particular prisoner of war and his other captive friends?

Read Daniel 2:48-49. List Daniel's role and that of his friends in these verses.

Reflect on your own life. Where has God given you some advantage or "favor" with others?

What other gifts or abilities has the Lord bestowed on you to use? (Daniel's included knowledge, understanding, the ability to learn, and the ability to understand visions.)

Describe a time when, like Daniel, God has given you unexpected wisdom to navigate a difficult situation or negotiate a solution:

Even though Daniel was a captive and a prisoner, God placed him in a position of power and influence. He made him uniquely able to do his job. Where have you been promoted to a significant position of leadership or influence? How can you be God's person in that situation, beyond thinking only of evangelism?

SPEND SOME TIME IN PRAYER thanking God for your situation, however difficult. Ask the Lord to help you be uniquely able to do what's needed in that place or situation.

REFLECT:

- Are you willing to respond with "Here I am" to anything the Lord asks of you, like Isaiah?
- Are you being called to be a mother, or father, or mentor to a people, like Deborah?
- Are you being positioned to become a political or national (or local) leader of influence, like Daniel (where, by the way, God redeems Daniel's abduction and prisoner of war experiences)?
- What do these stories seem to be saying to you, personally?

DAY FOUR   POSITION, PURPOSE, INFLUENCE

Queen Esther's Purpose

The Book of Esther echoes the same sense of destiny as that of Daniel. Esther, an orphan and a Hebrew, is chosen as Queen of all of Persia. (For more on the story, read Esther 1 and 2.) That in itself might seem like the end of the story. However, one of the king's key officials, Haman, plots to annihilate the Jews. Esther's Uncle Mordecai asks Esther to speak up on behalf of her people. Her initial reply is that she cannot without risk to her own life.

Read Mordecai's response in Esther 4:12-14.
What does he say to her about her purpose, her calling?

Where might you be tempted to rest in your currently-achieved position and not listen to God's nudging you to go the extra mile or do the next hard thing?

Where do you have a sense that you have come to your position "for such a time as this"?

Read Esther 4:15-17; 5:1-4; 7:3-5.
What does Esther choose to do—at risk to her own life?

Wall-Builder Nehemiah

Read Nehemiah 1:1-11.
Nehemiah was one of the Jewish exiles—people taken captive in the 5th century BC. Even as a foreigner, he managed to earn the influential and critical position as cupbearer to the King of Persia. The king's faith in Nehemiah is absolute, as he trusts Nehemiah with his life on a daily basis.

Where have you perhaps forgotten how important your daily or weekly role(s) are?

When Nehemiah receives the report about the tragic state of Jerusalem and of his fellow Jews, what are his responses (v. 4)?

What kinds of things does Nehemiah pray in verses 5-11?

Take some time now to craft your own prayer, modeled on that of Nehemiah—and pray it today about a specific situation where you are seeking God's influence and intervention.

Read Nehemiah 2:1-9. List the things that occur following Nehemiah's prayer in Chapter 1. For example: the king actually notices Nehemiah's sadness for the first time (v. 1-2).

Think of a prayer you have prayed recently. Can you list some things that have occurred as a result?

Read Nehemiah 2:10, 19-20; 4:1-23. Was Nehemiah's pursuit of and obedience to God's call easy? What kind of opposition did Nehemiah and the people face?

Where are you facing opposition to pursuing or completing something God is calling you to do?

Look back to the Nehemiah passages you just read. List some of Nehemiah's responses to the opposition.

Where can you do one or more of these things (literally or symbolically) to overcome resistance you are experiencing?

Note the ultimate accomplishment resulting from Nehemiah's prayer for Jerusalem and his people, his prayer to return, his willingness to lead, and his courage in facing constant opposition in Nehemiah 6:15. How long did it take a discouraged, disgraced, and unskilled people to rebuild the wall around the city?

Do you find that incredible? Where does it make you more hopeful of God's help in your situation?

REFLECT:

- Are you being called to step in and advocate for justice or to save a people (or a person) from destruction, like Esther?
- Are you in a position like cupbearer to a king, maybe in order to lead a significant effort like the rebuilding of a ruined wall, like Nehemiah?
- Pray today about what you sense God saying to you through these stories about your own story.

DAY FIVE CALLING AND IMPACT

New Testament Examples

Looking into the New Testament, the pattern continues of people being set apart, called by God to a particular role or ministry. Look up each of the following passages and fill in each person's calling and response.

Passage	Person	Calling(s)	Response
Luke 1:11-17; Mark 1:1-8	John the Baptist		
Luke 1:26-38	Mary		
Mark 1:16-20; 3:13-19; Mark 2:13-14	Jesus' disciples; Levi (Matthew)		
Matthew 16:17-20; John 21:15-19	Peter		
Acts 21:17-19; Romans 1:1-5; Romans 15:15-20	Paul		
Acts 13:1-3	Barnabas and Paul		
Acts 16:11-15; 40	Lydia		

Jot down one or more things that you sense God calling you to, nudging you to, or whispering to you about:

You may have noted along the way that people may have more than one calling. Paul considered himself called to Jesus, called to be an apostle, set apart for the gospel, called to preach the gospel to the Gentiles, set apart to plant churches, inspired to write letters encouraging those churches, etc.

REFLECT:

- Are you called to humbly prepare the way for someone else, like John the Baptist?
- Are you called to something improbably stunning and also impossibly difficult, like Mary?
- Are you willing to follow without knowing where God is leading you, like the disciples?
- Is your call to reach a particular people group for Christ, like Paul? Or to be set apart by your church for certain work, like Barnabas?
- Are you called to respond to the nudge of the Holy Spirit to open your home for a godly purpose…that might grow into something bigger, like Lydia?

Callings from God haven't stopped with the Old and New Testaments. Mother Teresa was first called to be a nun, then a school teacher, and finally to simply pick up and care for one dying person on the streets of Calcutta…which turned into serving "the poorest of the poor" (whom she saw as "Christ in a distressing disguise"), ultimately founding the order of Missionaries of Charity. Martin Luther King, Jr.'s call was to be a preacher and ultimately to advocate (and give his life) for equal rights for people of color through non-violence.

C. S. Lewis, who came to faith in Jesus later in life, was called to continue as a professor of English at Oxford University, to be a Christian apologist, and to write the seminal book *Mere Christianity* as well as the children's allegorical series *The Chronicles of Narnia*. God used all of his talents and training—present before his becoming a Christian, along with his newfound faith, to influence generations to think deeply about Jesus, Scripture, and the world around them. Lewis' good friend and colleague, J. R. R. Tolkien, author of the epic series *Lord of the Rings*, rooted his writing of fantasy in his Christianity to influence an increasingly secularized world.

Millard Fuller's desire was to eliminate poverty housing around the world which resulted in the founding of Habitat for Humanity. Clara Barton had a passion to serve God by serving wounded soldiers--first becoming a nurse in the Civil War, and ultimately founding the American Red Cross. Galileo, Isaac Newton, Blaise Pascal, and Francis Collins were not called to a pastorate but called to science—the solar system, physics, mathematics, genetics. Michelangelo, master artist responsible for painting the Sistine Chapel ceiling (The Birth of Adam), sculpting the Pieta and the David said, late in his life, "Many believe - and I believe - that I have been designated for this work by God. In spite of my old age, I do not want to give it up; I work out of love for God and I put all my hope in Him."[3]

Who would you add to this list - famous or not-so-famous?

Name one person you know who followed or is following a clear call:

It is not just the famous (or now famous) who are called. The comparatively anonymous or less-celebrated lives, by worldly standards, that most of us think we lead are equally subject to God's call. Maybe you are a company executive who is called to be ethical, fair, and a champion of diversity in your workplace. Perhaps you are a public school bus driver who warmly welcomes the children on your bus, silently praying for each one even though they are unaware of that quiet ministry. You might be called to adopt a child or foster a child with special needs. Maybe you are called to step out in faith and lead a small group of college-age adults, mentoring them through tough choices. Perhaps your calling is to be a good neighbor in your neighborhood, making yourself available more than most.

God's call can look like being a missionary or an evangelist for a living or it can be linked to your profession, your athletic ability, your vocational training, your love for math and science, your desire to write or create. The Lord can use anything—your talents, your expertise, your gifts, your interests, your past life experiences—to draw you towards how and where He wants to use you as a person of influence.

What do you really love doing or what do you believe you do well? List at least two things:

How has reading this diversity of callings or looking at your list of what you do well help to define one or more of your current callings?

Reflect:

● Are you called to be faithful as a school teacher? Or a hospice worker? Or as a missionary of charity, like Mother Teresa?
● Are you called to stand up for the rights of people of color, like Martin Luther King, Jr.?
● Are you called to serve as a doctor or nurse or caregiver to provide the best possible care for those who are ill, like Clara Barton?
● Or to mission work?
● Writing—fiction or nonfiction?
● Are you called to gain a better understanding of God's world as a scientist?
● The best artist? Company executive? Bus driver? Adoptive or foster parent? Mentor? Neighbor?

God promises to not only call and involve us, but to equip us to be able to do what He asks us to do. If you have some fear and trepidation around what God might ask of you, remember: He will empower you to do that very thing. And, oftentimes, He asks us to take a baby step forward—to commit to something small first. He will provide the power and the wisdom and the sustenance. The Lord does not leave us on our own.

REVIEW THE PAST FIVE DAYS OF HOMEWORK:
● From the Scriptures you read and your responses to the related questions, select one key lesson you learned.
● From the personal reflection questions, select one thing you learned about yourself, your call, or God's equipping.
● Transfer these two lessons learned to the chart on page 164.

SMALL GROUP DISCUSSION GUIDE FOR WEEK ONE

calling

If your group is meeting weekly, and each person is completing the five days of homework in advance, consider using this discussion guide to help with facilitating your conversation.

DAY ONE: NAMES, AGES, STAGES, HEARING

1. What stood out to you about the Lord's calling of Abram and Sarai and their response?
2. Do you believe that God can call you at any age/stage of life? Why or why not?
3. Where might you, like Samuel, need help in discerning God's voice?
4. Who might be your "Eli"—someone who can listen with you?

DAY TWO: LISTENING, RECEPTIVITY, RESPONSE

1. Is there a life pattern that points to the theme of your calling? If yes, what is it?
2. Where are you hearing God, but your excuse for delaying sounds a lot like "Lord, I'm afraid"?

DAY THREE: COMMISSIONING, ROLES, PLACEMENT

1. Where might you need to confess your shortcomings, guilt, or sins—things that are separating you from God and from hearing Him or seeing Him more clearly?
2. Where are you willing to say to God "Here I am! Send me"?
3. Where does it seem that God is at work in the roles you play?
4. Discuss the uniqueness of Daniel's situation and reflect on how God equipped, directed, and provided for Daniel.
5. Discuss: Where are you in a significant position of leadership or influence? How can you be God's person in that situation?

DAY FOUR: POSITION, PURPOSE, INFLUENCE

1. Where do you have a sense that you are where you are "for such a time as this"?
2. Discuss Nehemiah's prayer and ask someone to share the prayer they wrote, modeled on Nehemiah's.
3. Where are you facing opposition to pursuing or completing something God is calling you to do?

DAY FIVE: CALLING AND IMPACT

1. Spend time allowing each individual to share his/her current sense of God's call. If this is difficult, have each person answer the question: What do you really love doing or what do you believe you do well?

◼◀ VIDEO TEACHING

- What spoke loudest to you in this week's video teaching?

NOTES

VIDEO NOTES
calling and gifts

Week Two

calling and gifts

*C*alling involves being set apart by God and equipped by God to do His work in the church and in the world. Our exploration of call and use of spiritual gifts must be done in the context of God's design for the church being the Body of Christ. In part, our understanding is about finding each of our individual places in the body, hearing and living into God's call upon our lives, seeking His equipping, and embracing our own uniqueness. Beyond that, our comprehension and exercise of gifts needs to embrace the perspective that we are part of a whole - a Body - an organism, and that we are not given gifts in isolation. Scripture details everything from a collective call to a people (Israel, the church, all believers) to how God calls each of us in specific ways and then gifts us to do what He's called us to do.

THIS WEEK'S STUDY GUIDES

DAY ONE   UNIQUE, SET APART, MATURING

Read Psalm 139:13-16.
List at least five things this passage says about God's creation of you:
1.
2.
3.
4.
5.

Take a moment to reflect and/or journal your response to these concepts:

Read Jeremiah 1:4-5.
When was Jeremiah "set apart" for God's work?

What was the work God called him to?

Read Galatians 1:15-17.
When was the Apostle Paul "set apart" for God's work?

What term does Paul use in addition to being set apart?

Recall the work God called Paul to do:

How sure of it was Paul?

Think about your own life. Do you have the sense of being set apart by God for something?
Do you have an idea of what that something you are set apart for is? Jot down your thoughts:

If no, why do you think not? And, how might you seek and find that out?

Scripture says that you are "set apart." In what way(s) can you get closer to embracing that concept in your life?

Scripture is clear. Every person is uniquely designed by The Creator-God. Believers in that same God are also set apart for something uniquely theirs to do. Followers of Jesus have that same "set apartness" to God's work in the world. At times, it may be as clear as a call to work with a particular group of people or to a certain kind of vocation. At other times, we simply know that God does the calling and the setting apart, and we follow closely after Him to seek the where and to whom and when, being faithful in the other things we know He has asked of us in the meantime.

Read 1 Peter 2:9-10.

List at least four terms Peter uses to describe us—believers—as a group:

1.

2.

3.

4.

What is our role?

What are we "called out" of?

This role is a response to what?

There are over 800 references to "priest" in the Bible. Priests were consecrated and anointed to their work. They were to perform the various sacrifices required by God as atonement for the sins of the people—so that all might be forgiven and reconciled to the Lord. Theirs was a demanding calling, with rules about how they were to dress and how and when they were to carry out the sacrifices of animals, grain, incense, etc.

The book of Hebrews tells us that, in Jesus, we have our ultimate and final High Priest forever—One who ascended to heaven and constantly intercedes for us. We are no longer in need of the ongoing blood sacrifices at the temple—Jesus was the final blood sacrifice for our sins for all time. (See Hebrews 8-10.)

Think back to your reading of 1 Peter 2:9-10. Peter, under the influence of the Holy Spirit, calls us (believers in Jesus as Lord) God's "chosen people, a royal priesthood, a holy nation, God's special possession." In thinking of the Old Testament role of priest and now our role as priests to one another, what do you think being a priest to someone else might look like in your own life?

List at least two practical ways:

1.

2.

In addition to calling all of us priests, God also gives leadership gifts to some of His followers.

Read Ephesians 4:11-13.
What is the role of those who have these gifts?

Ultimately, what is the goal of leaders (equippers) in the church?

What has been your experience of leaders equipping you and others in your congregation to be the ones who *do* ministry?

List some things you think would be hallmarks of "unity of the faith."

List some things you think would describe "maturity—the measure of the full stature of Christ."

With this exercise in mind, on a scale of 1 to 10 (1 being not at all mature in Christ; 10 being very mature in Christ), rate yourself at this point in time:

	0	1	2	3	4	5	6	7	8	9	10
Not at all mature in Christ										Very mature in Christ	

END IN PRAYER, focusing on the thoughts in 1 Corinthians 6:11: "But you were washed, you were sanctified, you were justified in the name of the Lord Jesus Christ and by the Spirit of our God."

DAY TWO   UNIVERSAL CALL AND EQUIPPING

Universal Call

*W*hether you are clear or not on one or more of your callings, you can know that you are called to the following:

Passage	You are called to/set apart to:
1 Corinthians 1:1-2 …to those sanctified in Christ Jesus and called to be his holy people, together with all those everywhere who call on the name of our Lord Jesus Christ—their Lord and ours. **2 Timothy 1:9** He has saved us and called us to a holy life—not because of anything we have done but because of his own purpose and grace. This grace was given us in Christ Jesus before the beginning of time…	
Romans 1:6 And you also are among those Gentiles who are called to belong to Jesus Christ.	
Galatians 5:13 You, my brothers and sisters, were called to be free. But do not use your freedom to indulge the flesh; rather, serve one another humbly in love.	
1 John 3:1 See what great love the Father has lavished on us, that we should be called children of God! And that is what we are!	
1 Corinthians 1:9 God is faithful, who has called you into fellowship with his Son, Jesus Christ our Lord.	
Ephesians 1:18 I pray that the eyes of your heart may be enlightened in order that you may know the hope to which he has called you, the riches of his glorious inheritance in his holy people…	
Colossians 3:15 Let the peace of Christ rule in your hearts, since as members of one body you were called to peace. And be thankful.	
2 Corinthians 5:17-20 Therefore, if anyone is in Christ, the new creation has come: The old has gone, the new is here! All this is from God, who reconciled us to himself through Christ and gave us the ministry of reconciliation: that God was reconciling the world to himself in Christ, not counting people's sins against them. And he has committed to us the message of reconciliation. We are therefore Christ's ambassadors, as though God were making his appeal through us.	

These passages point to the sense of universal call—callings for all who follow Jesus. WE are individually and collectively called to be holy, saints, to belong to Christ, to be free, inclusive, peace and service-oriented ambassadors of reconciliation.

Review the above chart. Which area is it easiest for you to live into?

Which is most difficult?

Spend some time talking with God about this.

Read Hebrews 13:20-21.

Who equips us?

List at least three things that describe God or Jesus in this passage:
1.
2.
3.

What does this passage say God will equip us with?

What kinds of things do you think that includes?

How do you find these concepts freeing or encouraging?

SPEND SOME TIME THANKING, "the God of Peace" for equipping you with "everything good for doing His will."

DAY THREE   GOD AT WORK THROUGH YOU

Read Ephesians 2:8-10.
What does this passage call us?

Why does it say you and I were created?

Reflect on the implications of these verses for your life:

Read 2 Corinthians 9:8 in the NIV. Fill in the missing words:
"And _____ is able to bless you _____, so that in _____ _____ at _____
_____, having _____ that you need, you will _____ in _____ good work."

What does it look like for you to "abound in every good work"?

Read Philippians 1:6.
Whose job is it to complete our transformation to maturity in Christ?

Read 2 Timothy 3:14-17.
What does this passage say makes us wise?

List at least three things that our study of Scripture does to equip us for "every good work."

How have you experienced God's Word

- Teaching you?

- Rebuking you?

- Correcting you?

- Training you in righteousness?

These Scriptures and many others echo the Biblical theme that God is the one who equips us in every way. His call to serve and to use our gifts is one that presupposes that He is giving us what we need to respond to and carry out that call—in ongoing dependence on Him.

TAKE TIME TO PRAY Ephesians 1:18-23 NIV:

> "... that the eyes of your heart may be enlightened in order that you may know the hope to which he has called you, the riches of his glorious inheritance in his holy people, and his incomparably great power for us who believe. That power is the same as the mighty strength he exerted when he raised Christ from the dead and seated him at his right hand in the heavenly realms, far above all rule and authority, power and dominion, and every name that is invoked, not only in the present age but also in the one to come. And God placed all things under his feet and appointed him to be head over everything for the church, which is his body, the fullness of him who fills everything in every way."

DAY FOUR   LISTING GIFTS WE SEE IN SCRIPTURE

It is important to ground our understanding of gifts in Scripture—knowing what God has to say and desires for us. There are references to special giftings by God to His people in both the Old and the New Testaments. Most references come from the New Testament when God pours out His Spirit on believers in Jesus at the time of Pentecost and beyond. As you look at each of these passages, make a list of the gift or gifts you see mentioned (or implied), make note of the names of people it is said have that gift, and jot down anything else you find helpful from the passage:

Read Exodus 31:2-5.

Gift(s) listed in this passage:

Person/People mentioned with this gift:

Additional notes/further definition of the gift:

Read the following passages and see if you spot a theme that speaks of a specific area of giftedness in all of them--Psalm 150:3-5; Exodus 15:1, 20-21; 2 Samuel 6:14-15.

Gift(s) listed or implied in these passages:

Person/People mentioned with this gift:

Additional notes/further definition of the gift:

Read the following passages and see if you spot a theme that speaks of a specific area of giftedness in all of them--Colossians 4:12; Ephesians 1:16; 2 Timothy 1:3.

Gift(s) listed or implied in these passages:

Person/People mentioned with this gift:

Additional notes/further definition of the gift:

Read 1 Corinthians 12:7-11.

Gift(s) listed in this passage:

Additional notes/further definition of the gift:

Read 1 Corinthians 12:27-30.

Gift(s) listed in this passage:

Additional notes/further definition of the gift:

Read 1 Peter 4:9-11.

Gift(s) listed in this passage:

Additional notes/further definition of the gift:

Read Romans 12:4-8.

Gift(s) listed in this passage:

Additional notes/further definition of the gift:

Read Ephesians 4:11-13.

Recall the gift(s) listed in this passage:

Additional notes/further definition of the gift:

The importance of spiritual gifts

This workbook and its accompanying assessment identifies 23 gifts mentioned or implied in the Bible. Gifts are essential to the healthy functioning of the church. ALL need to be exercised in a spirit of love. ALL are given to individual Jesus-followers so that they might glorify God and strengthen the Body of Christ. Spiritual gifts are how God has equipped us to serve Him. God-given gifts make a far greater impact than simply using our own talents and abilities.

What is a spiritual gift?

Based on all the Scripture passages that talk about gifts, a spiritual gift is a unique ability given by God through His Holy Spirit to believers in Jesus—for the purpose of bringing glory to Him and strengthening His church. In addition, spiritual gifts are recognized and affirmed by the Body of Christ, and we see them evidenced in the life of Jesus and ministry of the early church.

Now turn to the next page to see how you did.

You may have noted the following gifts:

- ☐ Administration
- ☐ Apostleship
- ☐ Artistic Expression (You may have called this the gift of Praise and Worship or something similar; for our purposes, we will call it Artistic Expression.)
- ☐ Craftsmanship
- ☐ Discernment
- ☐ Evangelism
- ☐ Exhortation (sometimes called Encouragement)
- ☐ Faith
- ☐ Giving
- ☐ Helps (Some passages refer to this gift as "Service." We will use Helps as our term so as not to confuse it with the call upon all of us to serve.)
- ☐ Hospitality
- ☐ Intercession (that sense of constant praying and wrestling in prayer exhibited in the selected verses)
- ☐ Knowledge
- ☐ Leadership
- ☐ Mercy
- ☐ Prophecy
- ☐ Shepherding
- ☐ Teaching
- ☐ Wisdom
- ☐ Healing
- ☐ Miraculous Powers
- ☐ Tongues
- ☐ Interpretation of Tongues

You may wonder why take the time to search Scripture for a list of gifts. It turns out that the majority of those in the church, pastors included, have a tendency to confuse Fruit of the Spirit, spiritual disciplines, job titles, and talents with spiritual gifts.[4] These are each important, but very different from gifts in the lives of believers.

Keep in mind that a spiritual gift fits the definition of being a unique ability given by God through His Holy Spirit to followers of Jesus—for the purpose of bringing glory to Him and strengthening His church—a definition we find in the primary Scriptural passages about gifts (1 Corinthians 12-14, Romans 12, Ephesians 4, 1 Peter 4). Spiritual gifts are recognized and affirmed by the Body of Christ, and we see them evidenced in the life of Jesus and ministry of the early church. In addition, each gift may look quite different in each individual life. So we might say that there are twenty-three gifts—or, we might say that there are as many gifts as there are Jesus-followers.

DAY FIVE   YOUR GIFTS

God's call and our response

Spiritual giftedness is rooted in faith in Jesus. At Pentecost in Acts 2, Peter says "Repent and be baptized, every one of you, in the name of Jesus Christ for the forgiveness of your sins. And you will receive the gift of the Holy Spirit." God calls us to Himself. We acknowledge our need for Him and come to Him in humility and repentance, receiving His forgiveness and the promise of new life. That new life reflects God's call on the whole of ourselves (including both our natural talents and the giftedness we receive through the Holy Spirit), and we respond in gratitude and service to Him and to others.

We are TOGETHER the Body of Christ

Gifts are given to each of us to be used for ALL of us. The Scriptures that reference spiritual gifts do so in the context of a group. "Chosen people," "holy nation," "Body of Christ," "common good" are all plural terms that remind us that we belong to each other, and that gifts are to be used for others. Ultimately, our gifts are a way to steward what God has entrusted to us. What if most of us knew and lived out our spiritual gifts in the power of the Holy Spirit to the glory of God? What if our churches looked like a healthier Body of Christ, exhibiting broad diversity and uniqueness while living in unity, love, and peace?

God equips us with what we need to do His work

God does not simply call us to a life of generosity and service. He enables us to carry out His call through use of the gifts He gives us. As He promises in Hebrews 13:20-21, He will equip us "with everything good for doing His will." May the spiritual gifts assessment included here help you not only identify your God-given giftedness, but also start you on (or help you continue on) the journey of living into those gifts and further developing and using them. May you also discover new ways of affirming and embracing the gifts of others.

Completing Your Spiritual Gifts Assessment

When taking the following spiritual gifts assessment, please:

- approach it prayerfully, asking and trusting God to reveal Himself in the process;

- take it quickly; do not over-think the questions; write in the answer that first comes to mind;

- set aside enough time to complete it in such a way that it doesn't feel too hasty;

- be honest: you are answering how you are, how you behave, how you respond, NOT how you think you should be or how you think others view you.

You may also access a free online version of this assessment at:

GodGiftsYou.com

Your results will appear upon completion of the online assessment, with your top-scoring gifts listed first and your low-scoring ones last. Once you complete the online version, transfer your top 3-5 gifts and bottom 3-5 gifts to page 46 in this workbook.

Spiritual Gifts Assessment

Please read each statement carefully and give each one a score (from 0 to 5) relative to how well the statement reflects your behavior/experience. Answer how you ARE not how you want to be. Transfer the numbers to the boxes on the Spiritual Gift Assessment Scoring Sheet, page 45.

0	1	2	3	4	5
Never true of me					True of me

1. ____ I am good at taking care of details that other people might neglect.
2. ____ I have been successful in starting new ministries.
3. ____ God uses my artistic/musical gifts to help people worship him.
4. ____ I enjoy working with my hands to create things that facilitate my own or another's ministry.
5. ____ When I hear somebody claim to be teaching from the Bible, I can usually tell whether the teaching is sound or unsound.
6. ____ When I talk to non-Christians about Jesus, they are often interested in what I have to say.
7. ____ I am able to motivate others to persevere in the face of discouragement and struggles.
8. ____ I am more confident than most that God will keep his promises.
9. ____ I rearrange things in my life in order to be able to give my financial or other resources more generously to God's work.
10. ____ When there is a job to be done, I am one of the first to jump in and volunteer.
11. ____ In gatherings of people, I tend to notice those at the margins and make them feel like they belong.
12. ____ People who know me consider me a "prayer warrior."
13. ____ Others look to me for my knowledge of Biblical concepts and/or my insight into situations.
14. ____ When the path forward for a group is uncertain, people look to me for leadership.
15. ____ Comforting those who are suffering comes naturally to me.
16. ____ I often say things that people in the church need to hear, even though it may make them uncomfortable.
17. ____ I have been able to successfully guide others in their spiritual journeys.
18. ____ I can explain Biblical truth to people in a way that allows them to "get it."
19. ____ People look to me for counsel when there are decisions to be made.
20. ____ When I see people who are sick, I have a strong desire to pray for their healing.
21. ____ I have seen God do something miraculous in connection with a prayer I have prayed.
22. ____ When I pray, sometimes words come out that I do not understand.
23. ____ When someone speaks in Tongues, I am able to understand the message.
24. ____ Others look to me for my organizational skills.
25. ____ When I see a need in the church or community, I envision how to create a ministry to meet the need.
26. ____ I can communicate important things about God to others through creative writing, art, or music.
27. ____ I am skilled at creating useful items from tangible materials like glass, metal, wood, paper, etc.
28. ____ I can tell when there is spiritual evil in a situation.
29. ____ Sharing the Gospel comes easily to me.
30. ____ People think of me as an encouraging friend.
31. ____ In the face of doubt or uncertainty, I persevere in doing the things God has called me to do.
32. ____ I frequently look for opportunities to contribute money or resources in a way that makes a difference.
33. ____ I do not particularly care what I'm doing to serve, as long as it helps further God's work in the church or the world.
34. ____ Either in my home or elsewhere, I create a welcoming atmosphere for others.
35. ____ When I learn about somebody in a difficult situation, my first impulse is to pray.
36. ____ I see the shades of gray in situations where others see black and white.
37. ____ I motivate others to come along with me as I pursue God's vision.

38. _____ My automatic response when someone is hurting is to come alongside and offer a listening ear and a shoulder to cry on.
39. _____ God sometimes leads me to ask difficult questions and point out inconvenient truths.
40. _____ I enjoy coming alongside someone in one-on-one mentoring.
41. _____ I am able to connect God's truth with today's life situations.
42. _____ I can usually see the wise course of action to take.
43. _____ I have seen God heal someone in connection with a prayer I have prayed or by my laying on of hands.
44. _____ I have sometimes felt powerfully led by God to perform an extraordinary act.
45. _____ Praying privately in Tongues builds my personal faith and helps me feel closer to God.
46. _____ I am able to provide the meaning of a message of Tongues to others present.
47. _____ If somebody has a good vision, I can do the work of putting it into practice.
48. _____ I have been told I exhibit an entrepreneurial capacity.
49. _____ I express something of God's creativity through dance, imaginative writing, painting, drawing, or drama.
50. _____ Others depend on me to make or fix things.
51. _____ Others have told me that I have a strong intuitive sense, seeing dangers or opportunities that others miss.
52. _____ I actively develop relationships with and reach out to those outside the church community.
53. _____ I enjoy helping people take steps toward greater maturity in any aspect of their lives.
54. _____ In situations where others might doubt God, I do not.
55. _____ Although my generosity is usually meant to be anonymous, people know me as charitable and philanthropic with the resources God has given me.
56. _____ I enjoy doing the behind-the-scenes things that support others' ministries.
57. _____ Others have noticed that I am good at making people feel welcome and accepted wherever I go.
58. _____ I am one of the first people others turn to when asking for prayer.
59. _____ I often see important aspects of Biblical passages that others do not recognize.
60. _____ I inspire others to pursue goals that I clearly articulate.
61. _____ People describe me as compassionate and empathic.
62. _____ God uses me to point out his plans and purposes when others may be straying from the path.
63. _____ I find satisfaction in long-term coaching relationships.
64. _____ Others have consistently said that they have learned from or been challenged by my teaching.
65. _____ I am rarely confused about what next steps to take in challenging situations.
66. _____ I am drawn to participate in ministries like "inner healing prayer" or "spiritual deliverance healing."
67. _____ God has authenticated a message or ministry by working through me to perform something supernatural.
68. _____ I have spoken about faith in a language that is not my native tongue, and felt like God was enabling my fluency.
69. _____ If someone prays in Tongues, I get a feeling or vision or picture of what the message means.

(Transfer your scores for each question onto the scoring sheet on the next page.)

Spiritual Gift Assessment Scoring Sheet

- Please **record your scores** from the previous two pages onto this chart. Pay attention to the question numbering—it counts across, not down!
- Once done, **total each column** to get a number for each letter.
- Then, circle your top 3-5 scores (looking at A through W).
- Note your lowest 3-5 scores (just looking at A through S).
- Turn to the next page to find your corresponding gifts (and likely non-gifts).

1.	2.	3.	4.	5.	6.	7.	8.	9.	10.	11.	12.
24.	25.	26.	27.	28.	29.	30.	31.	32.	33.	34.	35.
47.	48.	49.	50.	51.	52.	53.	54.	55.	56.	57.	58.
A.	B.	C.	D.	E.	F.	G.	H.	I.	J.	K.	L.

13.	14.	15.	16.	17.	18.	19.	20.	21.	22.	23.
36.	37.	38.	39.	40.	41.	42.	43.	44.	45.	46.
59.	60.	61.	62.	63.	64.	65.	66.	67.	68.	69.
M.	N.	O.	P.	Q.	R.	S.	T.	U.	V.	W.

Spiritual Gift Assessment Results

Spiritual Gifts	Record Your Top 3-5 Scores (A – W):	List Your Lowest 3-5 Scores (A - S):	Which gifts do others affirm you have? (Ask a few people who know you well):
A= Administration			
B= Apostleship			
C= Artistic Expression			
D= Craftsmanship			
E= Discernment			
F= Evangelism			
G= Exhortation			
H= Faith			
I= Giving			
J= Helps			
K= Hospitality			
L= Intercession			
M= Knowledge			
N= Leadership			
O= Mercy			
P= Prophecy			
Q= Shepherding			
R= Teaching			
S= Wisdom			
T= Healing*			
U = Miraculous Powers*			
V = Tongues*			
W = Interpretation of Tongues*			

*See further explanation on page 53.

REVIEW THE PAST FIVE DAYS OF HOMEWORK:

- From the Scriptures you read and your responses to the related questions, select one key lesson you learned.
- From the personal reflection questions, select one thing you learned about yourself, your call, or God's equipping.
- Transfer these two lessons learned to the chart on page 164.

SMALL GROUP DISCUSSION GUIDE FOR WEEK TWO

calling and gifts

DAY ONE: UNIQUE, SET APART, MATURING

1. Discuss people's experience of responding to the concepts in Psalm 139.
2. Discuss what it means to be set apart for God's work.
3. If we are a chosen people, a royal priesthood, a holy nation, discuss some practical ways that can be lived out.

DAY TWO: UNIVERSAL CALL AND EQUIPPING

1. Have the group refer back to the Universal Call chart on page 33. Spend time discussing the implications of these universal calls on our lives as Christ-followers.
2. Reflect on the concepts that God will "equip you with everything good for doing his will" and will work "in us what is pleasing to him" (Hebrews 13:20-21).

DAY THREE: GOD AT WORK THROUGH YOU

1. Reflect on the concepts that you are "God's handiwork, created in Christ Jesus to do good works, which God prepared in advance for us to do" (Ephesians 2:10); that "God is able to bless you abundantly, so that in all things at all times, having all that you need, you will abound in every good work" (2 Corinthians 9:8).
2. How do you find these concepts freeing or encouraging?

DAY FOUR: LISTING GIFTS WE SEE IN SCRIPTURE

Hopefully everyone took the time to look up and become familiar with the list of gifts in Scripture. If not, turn to page 40 to review the list briefly.

DAY FIVE: YOUR GIFTS

1. Ask each person to list their 2 highest-scoring gifts and low-scoring gifts.
2. Note the diversity (and similarities) in your group's giftings.

◼️ VIDEO TEACHING

- What spoke loudest to you in this week's video teaching?

PRAY EPHESIANS 1:18-23 together as a group at the end of your discussion time.

"...that the eyes of your heart may be enlightened in order that you may know the hope to which he has called you, the riches of his glorious inheritance in his holy people, and his incomparably great power for us who believe. That power is the same as the mighty strength he exerted when he raised Christ from the dead and seated him at his right hand in the heavenly realms, far above all rule and authority, power and dominion, and every name that is invoked, not only in the present age but also in the one to come. And God placed all things under his feet and appointed him to be head over everything for the church, which is his body, the fullness of him who fills everything in every way."

NOTES

Video Notes

your spiritual gifts and the Body of Christ

Week Three

your spiritual gifts and the Body of Christ

You are unique

Throughout Scripture, God makes it clear that each of us is precious to Him, created uniquely and specially for a purpose of His design. We see in Psalm 139:14 that we are "fearfully and wonderfully made" by God. Ephesians 2:10 adds that we are "God's handiwork," created to do good.

You are set apart for God

As believers, we have become part of God's forever family: "…now your sins have been washed away, and you have been set apart for God. You have been made right with God because of what the Lord Jesus Christ and the Spirit of our God have done for you" (1 Corinthians 6:11). "You are a chosen people, a royal priesthood, a holy nation, a people belonging to God, that you may declare the praises of him who called you out of darkness into his wonderful light" (1 Peter 2:9).

You are called and equipped by God

You and I are called by God to do His work in the world AND equipped by Him to do that which He has called us to do. Part of that equipping is giving each believer in Jesus Christ spiritual gifts—special abilities empowered by the Holy Spirit—to accomplish His purposes and bring Him glory. Ephesians 4:11-13 says that gifts are given by God "to equip his people for works of service, so that the body of Christ may be built up until we all reach unity in the faith and in the knowledge of the Son of God and become mature, attaining to the whole measure of the fullness of Christ." We are not on our own in this. God will do His work in and through us, as we are submitted to Him and sensitive to His leading. Philippians 1:6 gives us confidence that God will complete the work that is begun in us.

This Week's Study Guides

DAY ONE   DEBRIEFING YOUR DISCOVERIES

*L*ist your top 3-5 gifts here:

Circle the one(s) that confirm what you already knew about yourself.

Put a question mark (?) next to any that are a surprise to you or where you are not sure you know what they mean. Why are they a surprise? What more do you wish you knew about them?

Which one(s) did you expect to see in your top 5 but your scores for those were low? Why do you think that is?

Gifts are not always synonymous with titles. Are you a teacher but do not test for the gift of Teaching? Think about your context. Are you in a context where the more useful gifting is actually Administration or Exhortation or Wisdom or Shepherding? Did those show up for you instead? Or are you a leader but do not seem to have the gift of Leadership? Is it really leadership you need for your context or Administration? Faith? Apostleship? Think more about WHAT you do…the role you play. Maybe part of this journey for you is to embrace the gifts you DO have and let go of the ones you thought you SHOULD have.

List the 3-5 areas where your scores are lowest (only looking at gifts A-S):

How might these lower scores show you your need for others?

Clarifying Some Things

If you expected to find a certain gift in your results, but your score was low, that could be for one of any number of reasons:

- Think about where your head and heart were when you took the assessment. It might be worth going back over the questions to see if you gave yourself an unusually high or remarkably low score for one question in a grouping.
- Were you really honest in answering, giving yourself not only 0's and 1's but also 4's and 5's?
- Ask yourself, is it maybe just a disappointment for you because you wanted that gift but in reality you may not have it?
- Could it be confusion between titles and gifts?
- No spiritual gifts instrument is perfect.

What if a gift showed up on your list and you think, "I do not have that"…or even "I do not want that gift"?

- Recall the definition of a spiritual gift as being something that God gives you, and God decides the who and the how. If you have been given a particular gift, He intends you to have it and use it.
- Is this a spiritual gift or is it a spiritual discipline that is so faithful in your life that you could have answered yes to all those questions? Review the questions and your scores and see.
- Ask friends and family who know you well--they can usually affirm and confirm; they can often see things you do not.

Think about gifts as an exhibition of the character of God. It can be small things done in the name of Christ just by you showing up. Do not compare with someone else with that gift because it will not look the same. This is God's plan for how to do church--*with* other people who are differently gifted.

In addition, the gifts given to people in a particular setting often match that setting. Think about your own ministry or church setting. Is there more of a certain gift in evidence? What might that mean?

Has God abundantly gifted your team/group because of a current or a future ministry?

What might the giftedness of your people tell you about possible ministry opportunities that you are currently not taking advantage of?

Think again about your own ministry or church setting. Is there a particular gift or gifts that appear to be missing in your mix of people? What might that mean?

If you have done a gifts assessment before, compare your previous results with this new set. What is the same? What is different? What do you think God may be telling you based on your current assessment scores?

Remember that clarifying and living into your gifts and call involves an ongoing process of asking the Lord for clarity. God honors that prayer every time.

About gifts T, U, V, W:

These last four gifts are in darker-shaded boxes for several reasons:
- In an assessment like this, it is difficult to provide three questions for these four gifts that cut across most people's experience of the gift. So, you may in fact have one of these gifts, but the three questions were less descriptive of your own experience of that gift.
- You may also have never had the opportunity to see if you have one of these gifts, so your score would likely have been a zero or quite low. That does not necessarily mean you do not have the gift.
- Some churches have lots of confusion about use of these four gifts or do not teach about them at all, so depending on your own religious history, that can impact your score as well.

What do your scores for Healing, Miraculous Powers, Tongues, and Interpretation of Tongues (Gifts T, U, V, W) perhaps tell you?

(Please also refer to the individual pages 94 - 101 for these gifts and Appendix A for more detail.)

Spend some time praying about your gifts:

--that God would help you embrace the gifts He has seen fit to give you,

--that the Lord would help you let go of the desire to have a different set of gifts,

--that His Spirit would empower you to use your gifts in new ways,

--that He would help bring clarity to your understanding of spiritual gifts,

--that God would help you see the ways that the gifts of others complement yours.

DAYS TWO & THREE GOING DEEPER

On the following pages (56-101), you will find descriptions of each gift, along with some negatives and a few suggestions of places to serve using each gift.

Become familiar with your own top-scoring gifts:

For each one of your top gifts, locate the two pages that provide more detail—and follow the instructions on those pages, which include:

1. Noting your gifts and their definitions.

2. Reviewing the questions on the assessment that pertain to that gift. When you reread those queries, see if something stands out to you about your use of the gift.

3. Does the additional list of words describe you?

4. In looking at the list of negatives, note the things that can happen if we focus on the gift and not the Giver of the gift or if we rely on our own strength and not that of the Holy Spirit within us. Do these describe you at times? Jot your thoughts in the space provided on each page.

5. As you peruse the list of possible ways to use the gift—think broadly: where could this fit in the church, in the community, in your workplace, in your neighborhood, in your home? Does this give you more ideas of how and where this gift might be called into play? What would you add to these lists?

Once you are finished exploring your gifts on the following pages, skip to Day Four on page 102.

ADMINISTRATION

Those with gifts of **Administration** bring efficiency and order to the church and to other organizations. These are usually the planners, goal-setters, or managers. They look for new ways to help groups of people and necessary tasks run more effectively.	This is one of my gifts _____ I am unsure if I have this gift _____ This is not one of my gifts _____
Questions on the gifts assessment that pertain to Administration:	Review each question and jot down what comes to mind:
I am good at taking care of details that other people might neglect.	
Others look to me for my organizational skills.	
If somebody has a good vision, I can do the work of putting it into practice.	
Some words that describe people with this gift:	Put a checkmark below if you feel the word describes you:
Organizer	
Planner	
Strategizer	
Developer	
Goal-oriented	
Efficient	
Potential negatives to this gift:	Check the ones that feel like particular warnings for your use of the gift:
Getting lost in the details and failing to remember the vision/mission/purpose.	
Pride in organizational skills instead of giving credit to God for the giftedness you exhibit.	
Relying on programs and projects at the expense of people and needs.	
Some possible ways to serve using this gift:	Check which ways to serve sound like a potential fit for you, or add to the list:
• Committee member or chairperson	
• Facilitator	
• CEO/COO	

• Strategic planner	
• Conductor and analyzer of surveys	
• Event organizer	
• Administrative assistant/executive assistant	
• Elder/trustee	
• Wedding coordinator	
• Strategic/master plan committee member	
• Anywhere!	

Quotations from individuals with this gift:

JB: "I love to organize people, ideas, information, projects. Being at the center of the hub and putting all the variables in place to meet a goal effectively and efficiently is my sweet spot."

SD: "I love bringing order out of disorder. God has made me good at seeing the things that need to be done to facilitate or carry out a project. Keeping lots of people and tasks on schedule is something I am able to do without loads of stress. I see this as both a leadership gift and as a support gift."

CB: "I have used my spiritual gift of Administration in helping with 'behind the scenes' activities both here at church and at other non-profits for which I volunteer. I may not be out 'front and center,' but I'm working to help the church/organization run more efficiently and effectively, which for me, is typically in the finance/accounting/budgeting area."

If you think you have this gift, write your own quotation (a description of what this looks like in your life):

Having reviewed this gift in detail above, who else do you think exhibits this gift?

Jot down your reactions/reflections here:

APOSTLESHIP

Those with gifts of **Apostleship** introduce new ministries to the church. These are people who blaze new trails, pioneer new endeavors, and step out into uncharted territory. They may have a great desire to reach out to unreached peoples, to establish a new ministry, and to spread the vision of the mission of the church.	This is one of my gifts _____ I am unsure if I have this gift _____ This is not one of my gifts _____
Questions on the assessment that pertain to Apostleship:	Review each question and jot down what comes to mind:
I have been successful in starting new ministries.	
When I see a need in the church or community, I envision how to create a ministry to meet the need.	
I have been told I exhibit an entrepreneurial capacity.	
Some words that describe people with this gift:	Put a checkmark below if you feel the word describes you:
Starter	
Entrepreneur	
Pioneer	
Risk-taker	
Adventurous	
Culturally sensitive	
Potential negatives to this gift:	Check the ones that feel like particular warnings for your use of the gift:
May get bored easily with existing ministries/programs.	
May always be advocating change and innovation without recognizing people's often limited capacity for change or failing to spot change exhaustion.	
Vision may conflict with that of other key leaders in the organization.	
Some possible ways to serve using this gift:	Check which ways to serve sound like a potential fit for you, or add to the list:
• Founder of a company	
• Short-term missionary	
• Long-term missionary	
• Planter of new church ministries	

• Planter of new churches	
• Starter of new community outreach/non-profit organization	
• Involvement wherever there is a need for a new ministry or a new approach to ministry	
• Vision committee member	
• Strategic planning committee member	
• Early adopter of new ideas	
• Inventor	

APOSTLESHIP

Quotations from individuals with this gift:

KV: "I have a keen desire to reach out to unreached peoples, to help establish new ministries, and to spread the vision of the mission of the church. I am most comfortable in settings that are culturally different than the majority U.S."

DS: "I think the gift of apostleship is about being compelled to break new ground and set off into new frontiers. I've been involved with 'start-up' ministries for most of my adult life, and still seem to find more to be part of. New churches, a church in a pub, new ministries, new classes, a neighborhood Bible study, a new institute and a new initiative are some of the 'new' that have formed my calling of apostleship. Nothing like the road to Damascus, but the continual goading of the Spirit moves me onward."

LS: "Learning that I have the gift of Apostleship has shed so much light on why I love to pioneer new places for the reach of the Gospel and justice for the poor and oppressed. This gift continues to allow me to naturally cross cultures and create new opportunities for movements, discipleship and sustained ministry, whether in the United States or abroad."

If you think you have this gift, write your own quotation (a description of what this looks like in your life):

Having reviewed this gift in detail above, who else do you think exhibits this gift?

Jot down your reactions/reflections here:

ARTISTIC EXPRESSION

The Spiritual Gift of **Artistic Expression** could also be called the gift of praise or worship. Those who have this gift have a special ability to communicate God's beauty, awesomeness, and message through the fine arts, including drama, creative writing, music, dance, and drawing. Through their God-given inspiration, these people use their gifts to draw us in so that we might focus on God, His creation and His message to us. Many with this gift speak of the sense of being compelled to use it in imitation of God the Creator and to show others how God is at work.	This is one of my gifts _____ I am unsure if I have this gift _____ This is not one of my gifts _____
Questions on the assessment that pertain to Artistic Expression:	Review each question and jot down what comes to mind:
God uses my artistic/musical gifts to help people worship him.	
I can communicate important things about God to others through creative writing, art, or music.	
I express something of God's creativity through dance, imaginative communication, painting, drawing, or drama.	
Some words that describe people with this gift:	Put a checkmark below if you feel the word describes you:
Artistic	
Expressive	
Creative	
Charismatic	
Original	
Innovative	
Potential negatives to this gift:	Check the ones that feel like particular warnings for your use of the gift:
Believing any public acclaim or attention is for oneself and one's own abilities.	
Craving the attention that comes with this gift.	
Focusing solely on the artistry and not on the purpose of bringing God glory.	

Some possible ways to serve using this gift:	Check which ways to serve sound like a potential fit for you, or add to the list:
• Worship team leader/member	
• Choral director/member	
• Drama team director/member	
• Orchestra/band leader/member	
• Artist/painter/animator	
• Singer/songwriter/soloist	
• Writer/author/journalist	
• Actor/actress	
• Choreographer/dancer	
• Videographer/photographer	

Quotations from individuals with this gift:

JB: "God has always been about creative communication! Angels appearing in the night, burning bushes, talking donkeys, you name it! As someone who teaches people how to make more effective presentations, I am constantly reminded how important it is to get myself out of the way! When I enter a workshop, completely open to whatever He may have me say and do, my class is ALWAYS wonderful. I am more creative, the class is more eager to tell me more about them, and the time together becomes time with Jesus Christ."

MR: "God has gifted me with a certain amount of creativity that I feel compelled to use, recognizing the Giver. This is played out in all aspects of my life, because it is deeply a part of who I am. Hopefully, my choice to live this out honors God, whether it is through a letter I write, a photograph I take, a conversation I have, a table I set, or a song I sing."

If you think you have this gift, write your own quotation (a description of what this looks like in your life):

Having reviewed this gift in detail above, who else do you think exhibits this gift?

Jot down your reactions/reflections here:

CRAFTSMANSHIP

People with the **Craftsmanship** gift are uniquely skilled at working with raw materials (wood, cloth, clay, paints, glass, etc.), helping to create things that are used for ministry or that help meet tangible needs. They might be found fixing, remodeling, and sprucing up buildings, and/or creating and stitching glorious quilts, pillows, wall-hangings–with the ultimate goal of honoring God and benefitting others. They view the use of their gift as a way of serving others in practical, hands-on ways.	This is one of my gifts _____ I am unsure if I have this gift _____ This is not one of my gifts _____
Questions on the assessment that pertain to Craftsmanship:	Review each question and jot down what comes to mind:
I enjoy working with my hands to create things that facilitate my own or another's ministry.	
I am skilled at creating useful items from materials like glass, metal, wood, paper, etc.	
Others depend on me to make or fix things.	
Some words that describe people with this gift:	Put a checkmark below if you feel the word describes you:
Creative	
Skilled	
Designer	
Practical	
Resourceful	
Capable	
Potential negatives to this gift:	Check the ones that feel like particular warnings for your use of the gift:
May fail to see the connection between this gift and God's purposes.	
May fail to recognize that their unique or exceptional skill at something practical is a spiritual gift and not simply a talent.	
Some possible ways to serve using this gift:	Check which ways to serve sound like a potential fit for you, or add to the list:
• Builder/repairer of buildings/facilities	
• Creator of banners, signs	

• Landscaper/gardener	
• Work crew member/craftsperson	
• Artist/painter	
• Crafter	
• Drama set builder/coordinator	
• Construction/installation	
• Interior design	
• Architect	
• Finish carpenter	
• Quilter/seamstress/tailor	

CRAFTSMANSHIP

Quotations from individuals with this gift:

KT: "I view my gift of craftsmanship as an ability to serve others through building (and repairing) things. I seem to be able to analyze a situation and devise a solution to it."

JF: "Craftsmanship is the result of having been given a compelling opportunity to design something that matters, defined by creativity. Craftsmanship showed up in the gifts of two of my all-time biblical heroes, described in Exodus 31:1-5 and 35:30-34. Their extraordinary gifts yielded craftsmanship, based on the Spirit's indwelling, wisdom, understanding and a keen interest in developing artistic skills, honed to benefit others, thus honoring God. When craftsmanship occurs in my life, it is because an artistic challenge has been met, inspiring a specific group of 'beholders,' hopefully including 'the audience of one.'"

If you think you have this gift, write your own quotation (a description of what this looks like in your life):

Having reviewed this gift in detail above, who else do you think exhibits this gift?

Jot down your reactions/reflections here:

DISCERNMENT

The spiritual gift of **Discernment** is the God-given ability, through His Holy Spirit, to distinguish between good and evil, truth and error, right and wrong, in a way that is helpful to the Body of Christ. These people provide much-needed insight, point out inconsistencies in the teaching of God's Word, challenge deceitfulness in others, and help sort out impure motives from pure ones. This gift can be an intuitive sense that something is not right either in the words or actions of others. It can help others sift through healthy versus unhealthy relationships and commitments, identify spiritual warfare and the activity of the enemy, and point out dishonesty.	This is one of my gifts _____ I am unsure if I have this gift _____ This is not one of my gifts _____
Questions on the assessment that pertain to Discernment:	Review each question and jot down what comes to mind:
When I hear somebody claim to be teaching from the Bible, I can usually tell whether the teaching is sound or unsound.	
I can tell when there is spiritual evil in a situation.	
Others have told me that I have a strong intuitive sense, seeing dangers or opportunities that others miss.	
Some words that describe people with this gift:	Put a checkmark below if you feel the word describes you:
Intuitive	
Perceptive	
Insightful	
Observant	
Aware	
Sensitive	
Potential negatives to this gift:	Check the ones that feel like particular warnings for your use of the gift:
Can be seen as being judgmental when pointing out what others fail to see.	
Can be inclined to be prideful in knowing right from wrong before others do.	
Can sometimes discern something that God simply wants to bring to their prayerful attention, but feel inclined to share it prematurely.	

Some possible ways to serve using this gift:	Check which ways to serve sound like a potential fit for you, or add to the list:
• Needed in all ministries and on all teams!	
• Counseling ministry/spiritual gifts advisor	
• Conflict resolution/mediation	
• Mentor/life coach	
• Adult Education teacher/Sunday School teacher/assistant	
• Elder/deacon	
• Personnel committee member/HR	
• Bible study leader/assistant/worship leader	
• Prayer team	
• Journalist	

DISCERNMENT

Quotations from individuals with this gift:

AH: "Many times, my gift of discernment is an intuitive response to someone in a committee meeting or something the group is pursuing. It doesn't 'feel' right. There is a built-in spiritual detector that goes off when something being said or actions to be taken do not seem right."

DB: "In my mentoring ministry, I have been able to help guys sort out right relationships from wrong ones, right career choices from bad ones, pure and holy motives from impure and sinful ones. I have been able to help other Christians identify, and deal with, deceitful motives, words and actions in their daily walk with the Lord. I have been able to identify, and pray for, situations involving spiritual warfare where Satan and his hosts are attacking a Christian work, witness or relationship."

If you think you have this gift, write your own quotation (a description of what this looks like in your life):

Having reviewed this gift in detail above, who else do you think exhibits this gift?

Jot down your reactions/reflections here:

Evangelism

Those with the spiritual gift of **Evangelism** are people who seem to always seek to build meaningful relationships with non-believers and are often able to steer conversations with these "neighbors" to spiritual things. They are enabled, in the power of the Holy Spirit, to communicate the good news of Jesus to unbelievers in such a way that they see people believe and commit to following Christ. These people just cannot not share their faith.	This is one of my gifts _____ I am unsure if I have this gift _____ This is not one of my gifts _____

Questions on the assessment that pertain to Evangelism:	Review each question and jot down what comes to mind:
When I talk to non-Christians about Jesus, they are often interested in what I have to say.	
Sharing the Gospel comes easily to me.	
I actively develop relationships with and reach out to those outside the church community.	

Some words that describe people with this gift:	Put a checkmark below if you feel the word describes you:
Convicted	
Forthright	
Persuasive	
Confident	
Approachable	
Heart for the lost	

Potential negatives to this gift:	Check the ones that feel like particular warnings for your use of the gift:
Can begin to think that people's coming to faith in Jesus is reliant on the skill of the evangelist more than on the power of the Holy Spirit.	
Can try to use this gift first in all situations when some situations might call for Helps or Mercy first and Evangelism second.	
Can force answers to questions hearers are not yet asking.	

Some possible ways to serve using this gift:	Check which ways to serve sound like a potential fit for you, or add to the list:
• Community volunteer/sports coach	
• Friend to an international student	
• Bible study leader	
• Drama team	
• Evangelistic team	
• Short or long-term missionary/missions committee member	
• Visitor calling team	
• Prison ministry	
• Vacation Bible School director/helper/Sunday School teacher/helper	
• Youth leader/assistant	
• Anywhere in the workplace	

Quotations from individuals with this gift:

BH: "Knowing that God has a purpose for everything, anytime I meet a person I think in terms of an opportunity to share Jesus' love and message. I try to talk, give an evangelistic brochure, or leave an open door for further conversation. I have seen many come to Jesus and there is no bigger joy."

LB: "I have a heart for people who may have been damaged by the church in their youth, and those who are turned off to Jesus because of the religious right. I love to turn their ideas of God upside down by presenting Jesus in a fresh, unexpected way. I spend most of the time listening, sometimes agreeing with them about the abuses they perceive, but then sharing what God has done for me. There is no arguing with that."

RD: "Good evangelists are people who engage others in conversations about important and profound subjects such as faith, meaning, hope, purpose, goodness, beauty, truth, justice and life. We work at being fluent in two languages; the language of the world we live in and the language of the Gospel. I find that I am more an interpreter/translator of the Good News. My challenge is to share the love of Christ in ways that address the head, the heart, and our imaginations."

If you think you have this gift, write your own quotation (a description of what this looks like in your life):

Having reviewed this gift in detail above, who else do you think exhibits this gift?

Jot down your reactions/reflections here:

EVANGELISM

EXHORTATION

The **Exhortation** gift involves offering a word of hope combined with a gentle push to action for those who are discouraged, tentative, or needing direction. People with this gift come alongside to offer reassurance and affirmation, and, when needed, to challenge or confront, all with the goal of seeing others grow to greater maturity. Exhorters, through the power of the Holy Spirit, can help people move further and go deeper than they would if left to themselves. These people help us go the distance and believe in our great value, even in times of challenge or personal attack. This gift is sometimes called Encouragement.	This is one of my gifts _____ I am unsure if I have this gift _____ This is not one of my gifts _____
Questions on the assessment that pertain to Exhortation:	Review each question and jot down what comes to mind:
I am able to motivate others to persevere in the face of discouragement and struggles.	
People think of me as an encouraging friend.	
I enjoy helping people take steps toward greater maturity in any aspect of their lives.	
Some words that describe people with this gift:	Put a checkmark below if you feel the word describes you:
Affirming	
Optimistic	
Reassuring	
Heartening	
Motivator	
Strengthener	
Potential negatives to this gift:	Check the ones that feel like particular warnings for your use of the gift:
Sometimes may only speak a word of hope in order to be liked.	
Exhortation may make the encourager attractive to others, causing one to forget that the gift is from God not the person.	
May be a person who needs much encouragement, so may get personally discouraged if they feel like the only one exhorting others.	

Some possible ways to serve using this gift:	Check which ways to serve sound like a potential fit for you, or add to the list:
• Counselor	
• Mentor/coach/spiritual gifts advisor	
• Sunday School teacher/Adult Education teacher/ Children's Church leader	
• Correspondent to missionaries	
• Stephen minister	
• Deacon/hospital visitation	
• Small group leader/assistant	
• Elder/support for pastoral staff	
• Anywhere in the workplace	

Quotations from individuals with this gift:

GB: "I see God using this gift when I have the opportunity to come alongside young women who are dealing with unplanned pregnancies. They do not get a lot of encouragement in their lives, so it is a blessing to allow God to work through me to build them up in a time when they feel so uncertain about anything. Even a little bit of encouragement goes a long way."

FB: "I have seen God use this gift to take people higher than they would have gone on their own. I remember the first time I recognized this gift was at a summer camp when I was a senior in high school. The entire camp was climbing up a mountain to a cross at the top, and it was not an easy hike. A lot of the people needed some serious encouragement so I was singing the whole way up and using 'great job!' over and over. By the time it was over, we had all made it up the mountain. That's the way I've seen God use this gift in my life, using me to help others get to the top of a mountain that they may not have made on their own."

If you think you have this gift, write your own quotation (a description of what this looks like in your life):

Having reviewed this gift in detail above, who else do you think exhibits this gift?

Jot down your reactions/reflections here:

FAITH

Having the gift of **Faith** is having that extra measure of confidence in God and His promises, helping inspire others to greater belief. Those in the church with this gift live constantly in the knowledge that in the midst of all things God works for good for those who are called according to His purposes (Romans 8:28). When others begin to doubt or flounder, these are the people who believe God is good, God is love, and God is fair, just, and merciful *all the time*. People with this gift obey God, take risks, and make sacrifices because they trust God completely.	This is one of my gifts _____ I am unsure if I have this gift _____ This is not one of my gifts _____
Questions on the assessment that pertain to Faith:	Review each question and jot down what comes to mind:
I am more confident than most that God will keep His promises.	
In the face of doubt or uncertainty, I persevere in doing the things God has called me to do.	
In situations where others might doubt God, I do not.	
Some words that describe people with this gift:	Put a checkmark below if you feel the word describes you:
Confident	
Believing	
Optimistic	
Hopeful	
Secure	
Convicted	
Potential negatives to this gift:	Check the ones that feel like particular warnings for your use of the gift:
Can lack empathy for those who doubt or whose faith is less strong.	
Can cross the line into "testing God."	
Can wonder why others do not act on God's promises as quickly, completely, or in the same way as they do.	
Some possible ways to serve using this gift:	Check which ways to serve sound like a potential fit for you, or add to the list:
• Anywhere in the church or the community!!	
• Bible study leader/helper	

• Elder/deacon/committee member	
• Youth ministry	
• Worship leader	
• Starter of new ministries	
• Missions team member	
• Adoptive parent/foster parent	
• Worker in an environment hostile to faith	

Quotations from individuals with this gift:

GO: "God's gift of faith enables me to accept His will for my life, knowing that He will work all things for good for me because I love Him (Rom. 8:28). As poet and artist Sister Corita Kent says: 'Believing in God means knowing that all the rules are fair and there will be wonderful surprises.'"

TV: "For me, having faith means never having to worry about anything. No matter how bad things may be in any particular moment, I have confidence that everything will ultimately be o.k."

If you think you have this gift, write your own quotation (a description of what this looks like in your life):

Having reviewed this gift in detail above, who else do you think exhibits this gift?

Jot down your reactions/reflections here:

FAITH

GIVING

People with the gift of **Giving** often do not themselves view it as a special "gift" and/or do not wish to receive public recognition for their generosity. They do not ask questions like "how much is too much"? In the power of the Holy Spirit, people with the gift of giving often view their resources differently–along the lines of "how much can I give away" and "how little can I live on to free up more resources for the kingdom of God"? They live as if everything they have belongs to God, knowing that God will provide for their needs. Giving may involve money as well as other resources like housing, food, clothing, etc.	This is one of my gifts _____ I am unsure if I have this gift _____ This is not one of my gifts _____
Questions on the assessment that pertain to Giving:	Review each question and jot down what comes to mind:
I rearrange things in my life in order to be able to give my financial or other resources more generously to God's work.	
I frequently look for opportunities to contribute money or resources in a way that makes a difference.	
Although my generosity is usually meant to be anonymous, people know me as charitable and philanthropic with the resources God has given me.	
Some words that describe people with this gift:	Put a checkmark below if you feel the word describes you:
Generous	
Self-Controlled	
Accountable	
Resourceful	
Sacrificial	
Steward	
Potential negatives to this gift:	Check the ones that feel like particular warnings for your use of the gift:
Can be too critical of what they deem extravagance.	
Can be seen as judgmental of those who do not also give generously.	
Can take undue credit for ability to earn/save more instead of seeing it as God's gifting and enabling.	

Some possible ways to serve using this gift:	Check which ways to serve sound like a potential fit for you, or add to the list:
• Donor to church programs and projects	
• Stewardship campaign chair/assistant/coordinator	
• Leader of and/or participant in courses on Biblical finance	
• Fundraiser/ resource-raiser for community or ministry needs	
• Debt-counselor	
• Financial advisor	
• Generous giver to community and other organizations	
• Host home provider for interns or missionaries	

Quotations from individuals with this gift:

GB: "Giving, for me, is really giving back to God in whatever way it is evidenced. A gift of my time, my financial resources, or my abilities seems small compared to the way that God has blessed me in my life. Decisions about what and how much to give tend to revolve around the need at the time, the best use of the resources I have, or the ways I see God working in me through that gift. Sometimes, the situation involves a strong need that I'm in a position to fill. Sometimes my particular abilities are a good fit for the need. Sometimes, a financial gift is a way for me to convert what I do well in my career into a means to fill a need that I can't fill directly through my abilities. Sometimes, I see myself growing through the decision to devote resources to God's kingdom. Often, that growth is only seen in the rear-view mirror of that opportunity. In all of these situations, it comes down to a willingness to be used of God in the entirety of my life, with my resources being a reflection of how God has gifted me, and gratitude for his provision in my life."

DK: "The foundation of Giving is the Truth that everything belongs to God to begin with, and He wants us to use what He has given to call attention to Himself--to honor and glorify His name. He has blessed our family richly in every way. The hardest part for me is Giving of myself to walk closely with Him, and to recognize His leading without always falling back into doing everything 'my way,' and trusting Him without feeling anxious about the future. Giving of financial resources is the easy part. We always have more than 'enough for every good cause,' and we pray that we can 'be generous at all times.'" (2 Corinthians 9:7-8, 11)

If you think you have this gift, write your own quotation (a description of what this looks like in your life):

Having reviewed this gift in detail above, who else do you think exhibits this gift?

Jot down your reactions/reflections here:

HELPS

The gift of **Helps** is one that meets the practical needs of others and of the church/organization in order to enhance, support, or accomplish ministry. One attribute of this gift is that many of these servants view "helps" as such a natural extension of who they are, they have a hard time acknowledging that it is an essential part of the Body of Christ. Other indicators of someone with the gift of helps are that he/she serves willingly, cheerfully, humbly, and wherever needed. They spot needs before others do and are sometimes surprised when other people do not notice the practical behind-the-scenes things that need doing.	This is one of my gifts _____ I am unsure if I have this gift _____ This is not one of my gifts _____

Questions on the assessment that pertain to Helps:	Review each question and jot down what comes to mind:
When there is a job to be done, I am one of the first to jump in and volunteer.	
I do not particularly care what I'm doing to serve, as long as it helps further God's work in the church or the world.	
I enjoy doing the behind-the-scenes things that support others' ministries.	

Some words that describe people with this gift:	Put a checkmark below if you feel the word describes you:
Supportive	
Practical	
Behind-the-scenes	
Humble	
Available	
Dependable	

Potential negatives to this gift:	Check the ones that feel like particular warnings for your use of the gift:
May not see their serving behind the scenes as a spiritual gift.	
May not value their gift equally with others' gifts	
May tend to say "yes" to too many commitments out of a deep desire to be helpful.	

Some possible ways to serve using this gift:	Check which ways to serve sound like a potential fit for you, or add to the list:
• Useful wherever help is needed!	
• Event set-up/clean-up/behind-the-scenes help	
• Coffee-time host	
• Communion preparer	
• Deacon	
• Usher	
• Food service worker	
• Nursery worker	
• Office assistant	
• Sunday School teacher and/or assistant	
• Stephen Minister	

HELPS

Quotations from individuals with this gift:

JK: "Using my gift of helps comes so naturally to me and is such a part of who I am, that I do not even think of it as a special gift. I find great joy in helping people when I can--sometimes to the point of 'over-doing' it. It has been a learning process for me to learn how far to go, as well as discern what kind of help is appropriate. Those of us with the gift of helps tend to see needs that are not so visible to others - and understanding this is crucial so that we do not become critical of people who seem not to notice the same needs which are so obvious to us. Taking the gifts discovery class was most enlightening to me because it pointed out why I am the way I am, and inspired me to use these spiritual gifts in new ways."

MD: "I have been able to use my gift of Helps in many ways - most recently in my role as Moderator for the Children and Family Ministry. This ministry is tasked with many duties and activities in order to care for and support children and families. My gift has enabled me to work behind the scenes as an extra pair of hands and feet to shop, cook, clean, assemble gifts, etc. so that the Director and her staff are free to achieve their greater goal. I truly enjoy being able to provide practical and necessary help and support, but the greater joy comes through seeing many gifts come together to bring glory to God!"

If you think you have this gift, write your own quotation (a description of what this looks like in your life):

Having reviewed this gift in detail above, who else do you think exhibits this gift?

Jot down your reactions/reflections here:

HOSPITALITY

Hospitality is the divine ability to make people feel welcome and accepted--anywhere at any time. Those with this gift enjoy connecting people with each other and creating an atmosphere in which relationships and community can flourish. Their graciousness and warmth make others feel cared for. And, as 1 Peter 4:9 says, they are the ones who do all this "without grumbling" or complaining.	This is one of my gifts _____ I am unsure if I have this gift _____ This is not one of my gifts _____
Questions on the assessment that pertain to Hospitality:	Review each question and jot down what comes to mind:
In gatherings of people, I tend to notice those at the margins and make them feel like they belong.	
Either in my home or elsewhere, I create a welcoming atmosphere for others.	
Others have noticed that I am good at making people feel welcome and accepted wherever I go.	
Some words that describe people with this gift:	Put a checkmark below if you feel the word describes you:
Accepting	
Welcoming	
Relational	
Safe	
Cheerful	
Warm	
Potential negatives to this gift:	Check the ones that feel like particular warnings for your use of the gift:
If undertaking too many commitments that involve hospitality, might burn out.	
Might not view this as a spiritual gift or as equally important to the Body of Christ as other gifts.	
Might wonder why all believers aren't more hospitable or as hospitable as the gifted one is.	
Some possible ways to serve using this gift:	Check which ways to serve sound like a potential fit for you, or add to the list:
• Greeter/welcome team/new member hospitality team/visitor calling team	
• Coffee-time host	

• Information booth staffer/coordinator	
• Small group leader/facilitator/helper	
• Friend to an international visitor/student	
• Host family for a church intern or missionary	
• Mentor	
• Host home for youth ministry	
• Stephen Minister	
• Anywhere in the workplace	

Quotations from individuals with this gift:

VH: "Cooking is not my gift so I was a bit confused as to why I had the gift of 'hospitality.' But the Discovery Class put it all in perspective. God was looking at my heart and not my cooking skills (or lack of). I may not love to cook but I love hanging out with people, and working with the Student and Family Ministries at the church has been a blessing and a complete fulfillment of that gift!"

MD: "I see it as a privilege to be gifted in hospitality, with the ability and desire to create relationships and the environments which foster them. Coordinating the New Members class was a great experience in using this spiritual gift, and I felt it. The work was some of the most enjoyable I've done, because I was serving within God's plan for me. Whether it was setting tables, calling volunteers, or planning menus, it felt right, fun, and worthwhile."

If you think you have this gift, write your own quotation (a description of what this looks like in your life):

Having reviewed this gift in detail above, who else do you think exhibits this gift?

Jot down your reactions/reflections here:

HOSPITALITY

INTERCESSION

Intercession–interceding, pleading, approaching God on someone else's behalf–is something we are all to do. People with this gift are those who feel compelled by God to pray on a daily basis for others. They are completely convinced of the awesome power and necessity of prayer. These are the folks you call first about a concern you have, because you *know* they *will* pray. Many with this gift are surprised it is a gift–they think ALL of us pray unceasingly as they do. They know that their faithfulness in prayer for others invites the power and the presence of God into every circumstance, and that prayer is not something to be taken lightly but is a battleground.	This is one of my gifts _____ I am unsure if I have this gift _____ This is not one of my gifts _____
Questions on the assessment that pertain to Intercession:	Review each question and jot down what comes to mind:
People who know me consider me a "prayer warrior."	
When I learn about somebody in a difficult situation, my first impulse is to pray.	
I am one of the first people others turn to when asking for prayer.	
Some words that describe people with this gift:	Put a checkmark below if you feel the word describes you:
Faithful	
Trusting	
Disciplined	
Consistent	
Spirit-led	
Steady	
Potential negatives to this gift:	Check the ones that feel like particular warnings for your use of the gift:
May not recognize that they have this gift since prayer comes easily to them.	
May wonder why others do not pray nearly as much as they do, and set themselves as the standard.	
May think that this gift is somehow less important to the Body of Christ than other more visible gifts.	

Some possible ways to serve using this gift:	Check which ways to serve sound like a potential fit for you, or add to the list:
• Prayer ministry/praying for individuals, family, co-workers	
• Prayer for missionaries and their families	
• Youth ministry prayer team/children's ministry prayer team	
• New Members ministry prayer team	
• Men's ministry/women's ministry prayer team	
• Prayer for pastoral staff and Session	
• Nursing home prayer ministry	
• Stephen Minister	
• Anywhere	

Quotations from individuals with this gift:

WN: "For me, the gift of intercession is an opportunity to call out to God and ask him to increase my faith and the faith of others to believe in a specific promise that God has given for a group or a person. It is also an opportunity to kneel alongside Jesus as He is interceding before the Father for the same thing, to follow and learn from him as He is interceding before the Father."

AB: "Prayer is a significant part of every day for me - blessing the kids as they head to school, praying the Psalms, interceding at work for co-workers, praying for needs and events I become aware of as part of [my church's] prayer ministry - and it always feels like a 'get to,' not a 'got to.' For me, praying Scripture is especially potent, and it is the main way God seems to speak to me."

JC: "When I intercede, there is a great peace and hope that comes from reflecting on our God, his might, power, compassion, and unfailing love, and then asking Him to become very real and evident to the individual and whatever they are facing. Since God is God and nothing is too hard for Him, it is encouraging to pray His kingdom come in the lives of others. The truth is there are some people God puts on my mind to pray for and I know he is calling me to pray."

If you think you have this gift, write your own quotation (a description of what this looks like in your life):

Having reviewed this gift in detail above, who else do you think exhibits this gift?

Jot down your reactions/reflections here:

INTERCESSION

KNOWLEDGE

Those with the gift of **Knowledge** bring Biblical truth and God-given insight to the church. Knowledge can look like receiving a word from God that is uniquely timed to and tailored for a given situation. People with the gift of knowledge may also be those who have a voracious desire to study and know God's Word, and God may use their deep understanding of Scripture to speak a word of knowledge to a person or group. They may be the ones who can see all sides of something and are able to point out the consequences or the forgotten details that others have overlooked.	This is one of my gifts _____ I am unsure if I have this gift _____ This is not one of my gifts _____

Questions on the assessment that pertain to Knowledge:	Review each question and jot down what comes to mind:
Others look to me for my knowledge of Biblical concepts and/or my insight into situations.	
I see the shades of gray in situations where others see black and white.	
I often see important aspects of Biblical passages that others do not recognize.	

Some words that describe people with this gift:	Put a checkmark below if you feel the word describes you:
Aware	
Truthful	
Perceptive	
Student of Scripture	
Attentive	
Spirit-Led	

Potential negatives to this gift:	Check the ones that feel like particular warnings for your use of the gift:
May be prideful of extent of knowledge.	
May be focused on analyzing and figuring out every situation, when sometimes what is needed more is listening or praying or trusting.	
May make Scripture study or seeking a Word from God the focus instead of God Himself being the center.	

KNOWLEDGE

Some possible ways to serve using this gift:	Check which ways to serve sound like a potential fit for you, or add to the list:
• Anywhere	
• Sunday School teacher	
• Adult Education committee member/teacher	
• Elder/Deacon	
• Bible study leader	
• Vacation Bible School leader/helper	
• Mentor	
• Strategic planning/vision committee member	
• Researcher/teacher/professor	
• Journalist/writer	
• Medicine	
• Committee member or chair	

Quotations from individuals with this gift:

AH: "I think of this gift in terms of being able to see all facets of an issue or subject, including important aspects that aren't immediately apparent. I also have to remember that Knowledge is different than Wisdom, and so the information I can bring to a situation needs others in the body who can decide how to use it wisely."

TC: "The gift of knowledge shows up for me first in a thirst to know more. I read the Bible usually everyday and then lots of commentary, and whatever else I can. If I do get anything from outside as a result, I get very clear images in my head at times."

FF: "While I am not a theologian, I have a hunger for learning and studying, going deeper, understanding in context, tying things together and then freely sharing in Bible studies. I memorize a lot of scripture which frequently comes to mind when needed most, and that's a great comfort."

If you think you have this gift, write your own quotation (a description of what this looks like in your life):

Having reviewed this gift in detail above, who else do you think exhibits this gift?

Jot down your reactions/reflections here:

KNOWLEDGE

LEADERSHIP

Those with the **Leadership** gift might be described as visionary, good motivators, and effective directors—helping lead and inspire others to achieve God's purposes. These people not only have it as a Spirit-empowered ability, but they also seek God's guidance and His will in their leadership and decision-making. Leadership involves not only having a vision of the preferred future for the church or an organization, but also having clarity on goals or next steps to achieve that vision, the ability to communicate the vision in a way that inspires others, and the ability to equip the rest of the team to pursue the direction together.	This is one of my gifts _____ I am unsure if I have this gift _____ This is not one of my gifts _____

Questions on the assessment that pertain to Leadership:	Review each question and jot down what comes to mind:
When the path forward for a group is uncertain, people look to me for leadership.	
I motivate others to come along with me as I pursue God's vision.	
I inspire others to pursue goals that I clearly articulate.	

Some words that describe people with this gift:	Put a checkmark below if you feel the word describes you:
Director	
Visionary	
Model	
Goal-oriented	
Persuasive	
Credible	

Potential negatives to this gift:	Check the ones that feel like particular warnings for your use of the gift:
Can be so vision-conscious that they forget the people-care piece of leadership.	
Can sometimes move too fast for their followers to grasp the need for changes, leaving them confused or weary.	
Can forget that Jesus' definition of a leader was as a servant.	

Some possible ways to serve using this gift:	Check which ways to serve sound like a potential fit for you, or add to the list:
• Elder/head of a ministry area	
• CEO/COO of a company	
• Vision team/strategic planning team	
• Committee chair	
• Ministry leader/coordinator	
• Sunday School teacher	
• Adult Education committee member/teacher	
• Worship committee member/worship leader	
• Manager/supervisor	

Quotations from individuals with this gift:

RD: "Leadership involves a vision of what goals you want the group to achieve, organization and planning to achieve those goals, and inspiration and equipping of the members of the group to participate in the planning and execution phases. I have been fortunate to have had leadership positions in both my job [at the university] and in volunteer work with the church, and what I have learned about leadership in each setting has helped in the other settings."

SA: "I see Leadership as the exercise of both insight and foresight - a leader sees more deeply than followers and helps them to see, and a leader sees further down the road than followers and acts on it. Insight and foresight are partly works of the Spirit, and yet can be developed by servant leaders - with God's help, one can grow in their ability to see. Some people call this vision and initiative - the ability to see things that others don't (in people, structures, and situations) and then do something about it. God often uses me to bring change - but the ability to see and act are the jumping off point for all leadership, it seems to me."

TF: "I am not always confident in my gift of leadership, but I find it very natural to lead other men in spiritual discussions, and to explore spiritual growth, especially when we are focused on real-life issues. God always gives me confidence in these times."

If you think you have this gift, write your own quotation (a description of what this looks like in your life):

Having reviewed this gift in detail above, who else do you think exhibits this gift?

Jot down your reactions/reflections here:

LEADERSHIP

MERCY

People who exhibit high levels of compassion, concern, care, and kindness are likely those with the God-given gift of **Mercy**. People with this gift gently come alongside others who are in pain, in need, or are lonely. God's grace and love is shown in practical ways through this gift. The mercy gift is one of comfort, support, and presence with those who are suffering, in crisis, or otherwise hurting. Those with this gift reach out to others who are broken, having themselves experienced God in their own brokenness. They show God's heart to those who need the empathy of a listening ear and human company.	This is one of my gifts _____ I am unsure if I have this gift _____ This is not one of my gifts _____
Questions on the assessment that pertain to Mercy:	Review each question and jot down what comes to mind:
Comforting those who are suffering comes naturally to me.	
My automatic response when someone is hurting is to come alongside and offer a listening ear and a shoulder to cry on.	
People describe me as compassionate and empathic.	
Some words that describe people with this gift:	Put a checkmark below if you feel the word describes you:
Caring	
Compassionate	
Loving	
Approachable	
Kind	
Gentle	
Potential negatives to this gift:	Check the ones that feel like particular warnings for your use of the gift:
Can wear out if there are no boundaries or limits on commitments that demand lots of energy and resources.	
May not see this as a unique gift they have, assuming all in the Body of Christ think and act as they do.	
May be taken advantage of by those who are manipulative.	

Some possible ways to serve using this gift:	Check which ways to serve sound like a potential fit for you, or add to the list:
• Deacon	
• Counselor/counseling ministry/mentor	
• Hospital visitation/prison ministry/victim advocate	
• Nursery/preschool teacher/assistant/Sunday School teacher	
• Stephen Minister	
• Ministry to seniors	
• Pregnancy center worker	
• Anywhere there are people in need—family, friends, neighbors, co-workers	

Quotations from individuals with this gift:

NB: "This gift drew me to serve as a victim's advocate with the police department. It was the desire to offer comfort, support, and to be present with people when they were in the midst of an emotionally painful event in their lives."

MH: "I always try to put myself in someone else's shoes. Thus, I can often see why one did something or said something because of his/her circumstances, and thus I am able to forgive or love a person who probably does not feel like they should be forgiven or loved."

SD: "The best way that I know how to describe mercy and how I use it in my life is: Meeting someone where they are with what they need."

JC: "It is God who dumps mercy on me the whole day long. He never stops the mercy river; my job is to transfer it to the next person in line."

If you think you have this gift, write your own quotation (a description of what this looks like in your life):

Having reviewed this gift in detail above, who else do you think exhibits this gift?

Jot down your reactions/reflections here:

MERCY

PROPHECY

Prophecy is a gift that God uses to convict His people of sin and their need for repentance. This gift is a Holy-Spirit-empowered ability to speak God's Word—truth—into a situation, calling people to turn back to God, warning of the consequences of not doing so, and reminding people of God's promises and of His justice and judgment. Knowing the right timing to speak a word from God depends on the person with the gift of prophecy being prayerful and sensitive to the Spirit's leading.	This is one of my gifts _____ I am unsure if I have this gift _____ This is not one of my gifts _____
Questions on the assessment that pertain to Prophecy:	Review each question and jot down what comes to mind:
I often say things that people in the church need to hear, even though it may make them uncomfortable.	
God sometimes leads me to ask difficult questions and point out inconvenient truths.	
God uses me to point out his plans and purposes when others may be straying from the path.	
Some words that describe people with this gift:	Put a checkmark below if you feel the word describes you:
Reveals	
Exposes	
Challenges	
Bold	
Warns	
Discerns	
Potential negatives to this gift:	Check the ones that feel like particular warnings for your use of the gift:
Sometimes people with this gift deliver the message harshly.	
People with this gift can get frustrated that listeners do not hear God's message and repent.	
People with this gift can feel rejected and be tempted to either stop speaking or to leave the church.	

Some possible ways to serve using this gift:	Check which ways to serve sound like a potential fit for you, or add to the list:
• Adult Education teacher/Bible study leader/assistant/ Sunday School teacher	
• Elder/preacher/worship leader	
• Prayer team member/coordinator	
• Prison ministry	
• Spiritual gifts advisor/ mentor/coach/counseling ministry	
• Youth leader	
• Anywhere	

Quotations from individuals with this gift:

KF: "I do have the gift of prophecy....much to my family's dismay! Everyone loves the person with the gift of prophecy who uses it to encourage and to shed light on a situation, the person who acts as a cheerleader ...but when it comes to being an instrument for God convicting others of the need to repent and change their ways---like John the Baptist--- or to rise up higher in their walk with Him, both the messenger and the message can be less enthusiastically received!"

LP: "In all honesty, I suppose it's the gift that feels most uncomfortable to talk about because it seems so...well, bossy. In the mix of gifts that God has given me, Prophecy seems to work in partnership with Teaching and Discernment. The mix of prophecy and discernment shows up in how I view the communities I'm involved in. Often I'll see needs or gaps in how that community is functioning--for example, in my family, I'm generally the one who identifies areas where we can work together more effectively or improve how we relate to each other. In my work, I sometimes see future directions in education that would help our program. The teaching gift then kicks in and prompts me to suggest courses of action. In a healthy community, I think Prophecy should be weighed against the wisdom of Scripture and/or the broader communal wisdom so that the ideas/practices that come from it are confirmed."

JK: "With some people, I have a knack for 'speaking forth' and helping them decipher God's intents and purposes in their life...even if they resist (which is how people often respond to prophets!). I have some reluctance in embracing the 'prophet' label because of the misconception of predicting the future, but I have recognized that God has given me unique access and connections to so many people who seem willing to open up to me, which then enables me to 'speak forth' key aspects of God's will in their lives."

If you think you have this gift, write your own quotation (a description of what this looks like in your life):

Having reviewed this gift in detail above, who else do you think exhibits this gift?

Jot down your reactions/reflections here:

PROPHECY

SHEPHERDING

Shepherding involves nurture and guidance of others so that they grow in spiritual maturity and Christ-like character. Some, but not all, pastors have the spiritual gift of shepherding; many others in the church also have this gift. Jesus was the Good Shepherd—He loved, protected, cared for, and led His sheep into life abundant. People with the shepherding gift seek to do the same by walking alongside someone for a long or short season and directing them to Jesus and His offer of life, hope, and peace.	This is one of my gifts _____ I am unsure if I have this gift _____ This is not one of my gifts _____
Questions on the assessment that pertain to Shepherding:	Review each question and jot down what comes to mind:
I have been able to successfully guide others in their spiritual journeys.	
I enjoy coming alongside someone in one-on-one mentoring.	
I find satisfaction in long-term coaching relationships.	
Some words that describe people with this gift:	Put a checkmark below if you feel the word describes you:
Fosters health	
Guide	
Counselor	
Model	
Trustworthy	
Supportive	
Potential negatives to this gift:	Check the ones that feel like particular warnings for your use of the gift:
Might begin to think/hope that followers are dependent on him/her instead of giving glory to God for the gift of Shepherding.	
May have a tendency to rely on own human wisdom instead of asking God for guidance.	
May have a difficult time ending a shepherding relationship when it is time for closure.	

Some possible ways to serve using this gift:	Check which ways to serve sound like a potential fit for you, or add to the list:
• Counseling ministry/mentor/coach	
• Deacon/elder/pastor	
• Bible study/small group leader/assistant	
• Sunday School/Adult Education teacher	
• Hospital visitation	
• Singles/Women's/Men's ministry	
• Youth leader	
• Stephen Minister	
• Life coach	
• Manager/supervisor	

Quotations from individuals with this gift:

DM: "Over the years, I have enjoyed the guidance, instruction, nurturing and fellowship of others who have shepherded me. God placed these special people in my life to be my role models. Today, I am counted as a shepherd in God's kingdom, and it is humbling indeed. None of my success in keeping watch over the 3rd graders in Sunday school comes from me alone. It is by His equipping that I take responsibility for the teaching of His word and the nurturing of these children."

RD: "I don't see myself as a shepherd of a large class of people or even a small group. But I do believe that God asks me to care for and guide those he has put in my path. I have been blessed with church positions that put me in contact with young interns, volunteer leaders and also those who are somewhat compromised (mentally or financially). The Lord has given me compassion for these people and I enjoy pointing them to Jesus. I enjoy loving others and helping them to see what the Bible says about their situation, and helping them to live fully in their new life in Jesus! I enjoy challenging people to deepen their relationship with Jesus through prayer and the power of the Holy Spirit. I try to speak love to those whom the Lord has brought me."

KB: "I see this gift used in my life through relationships with family, friends, and through discipleship. Many come to me seeking advice and help with decision-making, faith questions, and a desire to know Christ more.

If you think you have this gift, write your own quotation (a description of what this looks like in your life):

Having reviewed this gift in detail above, who else do you think exhibits this gift?

Jot down your reactions/reflections here:

SHEPHERDING

TEACHING

The gift of **Teaching** involves studying, understanding, explaining, and applying Scripture's truths in such a way that people grow in their own understanding, are challenged, and are inspired to apply what they've learned. This can be done in a church or other context, since God's truth is true everywhere. Those who have this gift teach with authority, relevance, insight, and stimulate the hearers, through the work of the Spirit, so they are motivated to learn, understand and apply what they hear.	This is one of my gifts _____ I am unsure if I have this gift _____ This is not one of my gifts _____
Questions on the assessment that pertain to Teaching:	Review each question and jot down what comes to mind:
I can usually explain Biblical truth to people in a way that allows them to "get it."	
I am able to connect God's truth with today's life situations.	
Others have consistently said that they have learned from or been challenged by my teaching.	
Some words that describe people with this gift:	Put a checkmark below if you feel the word describes you:
Communicator	
Instructor	
Accurate	
Thorough	
Insightful	
Inspiring	
Potential negatives to this gift:	Check the ones that feel like particular warnings for your use of the gift:
May see teaching as only a talent or skill instead of recognizing it being enabled by the power of the Holy Spirit.	
May become prideful in the attention received or results seen.	
May use the gift in inappropriate settings—where people might need mercy, hospitality, intercession, etc. instead.	

TEACHING

Some possible ways to serve using this gift:	Check which ways to serve sound like a potential fit for you, or add to the list:
• Sunday School/Vacation Bible School teacher/assistant	
• Adult Education teacher/Bible study leader	
• Mentor/coach	
• Preacher	
• School teacher/educator/professor	
• Worship leader	
• Youth ministry	
• In one-on-one settings	

Quotations from individuals with this gift:

NK: "I believe that the gift of teaching has manifested in such a way that I have increased patience, compassion and creativity. With this, I am humbled to reach out and help empower children to see their own gifts."

SB: "I facilitate a group that includes one Jewish woman, one skeptic, one atheist, and five Christians of mixed denominations. Our practice is to study a book of the Bible, gather for an hour, take turns reading out loud, and pause to reflect. I prepare ahead of time with historical or theological frames of reference that I offer in hopes of deepening their understanding of the passage. There is always an opportunity for the women to share out of their lives. I am not sure how to capture in words this wonderful thing that has happened with these women. I use this gift of teaching to open the Word of God to others so that they, too, can behold him, Father, Son and Spirit. I try to create thin places where he can make himself known."

WA: "Through the spiritual gift of teaching, the Holy Spirit 'reveals all things' to the Body of Christ by providing insights through a willing communicator. Knowing that the Holy Spirit will provide these insights frees me to serve as a class or small group leader."

KG: "Having the gift of teaching allows me to naturally teach the gospel and other truth to those around me. I see this gift at work in my friendships, my ministry to college women, and my job in children and family ministry."

If you think you have this gift, write your own quotation (a description of what this looks like in your life):

Having reviewed this gift in detail above, who else do you think exhibits this gift?

Jot down your reactions/reflections here:

TEACHING

WISDOM

WISDOM

Those with the gift of **Wisdom** use God-given direction and information and apply it, providing guidance to individuals and the church. People with this gift typically can see the right course of action in the midst of otherwise confusing or overwhelming circumstances that paralyze others. Often, input from those with wisdom can shift a group's direction or help guide someone toward greater clarity. The use of the gift of wisdom is less about authority and more about humility—rooted in truth and the guidance of the Spirit, which others usually recognize as such.	This is one of my gifts _____ I am unsure if I have this gift _____ This is not one of my gifts _____

Questions on the assessment that pertain to Wisdom:	Review each question and jot down what comes to mind:
People look to me for counsel when there are decisions to be made.	
I can usually see the wise course of action to take.	
I am rarely confused about what next steps to take in challenging situations.	

Some words that describe people with this gift:	Put a checkmark below if you feel the word describes you:
Guide	
Perceptive	
Spirit-led	
Astute	
Good judgment	
Insightful	

Potential negatives to this gift:	Check the ones that feel like particular warnings for your use of the gift:
Can begin to have pride that people seek him/her out for advice.	
Can begin to think the gift is infallible—that he/she is always right.	
May have a hard time following a leader who ignores what he/she says.	

Some possible ways to serve using this gift:	Check which ways to serve sound like a potential fit for you, or add to the list:
• Needed in all ministry areas and on all teams!	
• Adult Education teacher	

• Sunday School teacher	
• Elder/Deacon	
• Finance committee member	
• Prayer team	
• Spiritual gifts advisor	
• Counseling ministry	
• Personnel committee member	
• Stephen Minister	
• Strategic planning committee member	
• At home, at work, with neighbors, etc.	

Quotations from individuals with this gift:

KM: "I've experienced several exciting occasions when a single comment, by me or another member of a group, has moved a discussion in an unexpected, very productive direction or crystallized the group's thinking into clarity and solution. The circumstances I'm thinking of had nothing to do with the force of the speaker's personality and everything to do with what listeners recognized as truth and rightness in their words."

SD: "Part of how I know I have this gift is that people regularly seek me out asking for wise advice or perspective. Part of wisdom, too, is knowing when to share that advice and when to draw the wisdom out of others so they come to the conclusion on their own. I often have clarity with regard to next steps with individuals, in meetings, and in group settings when the individuals or groups do not."

If you think you have this gift, write your own quotation (a description of what this looks like in your life):

Having reviewed this gift in detail above, who else do you think exhibits this gift?

Jot down your reactions/reflections here:

WISDOM

HEALING

The gift of **Healing** follows the pattern we see in the life and ministry of Jesus where healing was physical, mental, emotional, and/or spiritual. Often in Scripture healing is used by God to pour grace upon someone while simultaneously authenticating a message or a ministry. Always it is to show God's mercy and power. Sometimes healing is instant and sometimes it happens over time. Our God is a God of restoration and wholeness, and healing is one way in which we see Him reach deeply into individual lives.	This is one of my gifts _____ I am unsure if I have this gift _____ This is not one of my gifts _____
Questions on the assessment that pertain to Healing:	Review each question and jot down what comes to mind:
When I see people who are sick, I have a strong desire to pray for their healing.	
I have seen God heal someone in connection with a prayer I have prayed or by my laying on of hands.	
I am drawn to participate in ministries like "inner healing prayer" or "spiritual deliverance healing."	
Some words that describe people with this gift:	Put a checkmark below if you feel the word describes you:
Restorer	
Intercessor	
Responsive	
Compassionate	
Spirit-led	
Alert	
Potential negatives to this gift:	Check the ones that feel like particular warnings for your use of the gift:
May be tempted to focus on the gift and not the Giver of the gift.	
May develop pride in the ability to heal.	
Mail fail to remember that healing is up to God and may not "work" every time it is called upon.	

HEALING

Some possible ways to serve using this gift:	Check which ways to serve sound like a potential fit for you, or add to the list:
• Healing prayer team	
• Prayer team	
• Prayer for individuals as God leads	
• Counselor/psychiatrist	
• Medical professional/doctor/nurse	
• Physical therapist/occupational therapist	
• Anywhere!	

Quotations from individuals with this gift:

AM: "I do not have any idea why God heals some people and not others. It is a mystery. I believe firmly in divine healing. I've seen it happen. I've even experienced it myself! Yet I am always surprised when God chooses to heal. Evidence of doubt? Not at all. It is delight--dancing-with-God in witnessing the mystery all over again. So I will continue praying for healing when the opportunities present themselves and joyfully embrace the surprise when I'm reminded of the mysteries of God!"

BR: "I work as a counselor, and my life verse is Isaiah 58:12 'Your people will rebuild the ancient ruins and will raise up the age-old foundations; you will be called Repairer of Broken Walls, Restorer of Streets with Dwellings.' This is how I view my work as a ministry of healing."

If you think you have this gift, write your own quotation (a description of what this looks like in your life):

Having reviewed this gift in detail above, who else do you think exhibits this gift?

Jot down your reactions/reflections here:

HEALING

MIRACULOUS POWERS

Miraculous powers (the ability to perform miracles) are given to individuals in the Body of Christ to authenticate a ministry, encourage a body of believers, and to show the power of God. In the life and ministry of Jesus, His miracles included feeding the multitudes, turning water into wine, raising the dead and walking on water.	This is one of my gifts _____ I am unsure if I have this gift _____ This is not one of my gifts _____

Questions on the assessment that pertain to Miraculous Powers:	Review each question and jot down what comes to mind:
I have seen God do something miraculous in connection with a prayer I have prayed.	
I have sometimes felt powerfully led by God to perform an extraordinary act.	
God has authenticated a message or a ministry by working through me to perform something supernatural.	

Some words that describe people with this gift:	Put a checkmark below if you feel the word describes you:
Authentic	
God-glorifying	
Faithful	
Spirit-sensitive	
Alert	
Courageous	

Potential negatives to this gift:	Check the ones that feel like particular warnings for your use of the gift:
May be tempted to focus on the gift and not the Giver of the gift.	
May develop pride in the ability to perform miracles.	
Can want to demand that God do something or repeat a previous miracle.	

Some possible ways to serve using this gift:	Check which ways to serve sound like a potential fit for you, or add to the list:
• Anywhere God directs	

A quote from someone with this gift:

CC: "I do think that healing and miraculous powers can be combined. I have seen these works performed and have performed them when I knew the Holy Spirit was VERY active in me. I want to be able to heal more, but only God knows when I will be able to—probably when I can 'totally' get out of myself and be in God and He in me."

PP: "When I took this gifts assessment two years ago, I tested for the gift of Miraculous Powers for the first time. I did not want this new gift at this stage of my life. However, in the last year, as part of our church's prayer team, and specifically in ministry outreach to those in crisis, I've experienced God doing the miraculous through me in these settings more than I ever have. I am excited to have this gift!"

If you think you have this gift, write your own quotation (a description of what this looks like in your life):

Having reviewed this gift in detail above, who else do you think exhibits this gift?

Jot down your reactions/reflections here:

MIRACULOUS POWERS

TONGUES

Those with the gift of **Tongues** may speak in other languages as the Spirit enables them (Acts 2); may speak in an unknown language (that of "angels"-1 Cor. 13); may speak to God in tongues (1 Cor. 14). Scripture says in addition to tongues being other languages, it is also a way of "uttering the mysteries of the Spirit" and "sounding a clear call" to God's people (1 Cor. 14). To be understood by the Body, tongues must be accompanied by the gift of Interpretation of Tongues.	This is one of my gifts _____ I am unsure if I have this gift _____ This is not one of my gifts _____
Questions on the assessment that pertain to Tongues:	Review each question and jot down what comes to mind:
When I pray, sometimes words come out that I do not understand.	
Praying privately in tongues builds my personal faith and helps me feel closer to God.	
I have spoken about faith in a language that is not my native tongue, and felt like God was enabling my fluency.	
Some words that describe people with this gift:	Put a checkmark below if you feel the word describes you:
Responsive	
Spirit-led	
God-glorifying	
Communicator	
Expressive	
Worshipful	
Potential negatives to this gift:	Check the ones that feel like particular warnings for your use of the gift:
May want to use it in all settings whether or not appropriate.	
May use it in public without an interpreter present which simply calls attention to the speaker but not the message of God.	
May be disruptive in worship.	

Some possible ways to serve using this gift:	Check which ways to serve sound like a potential fit for you, or add to the list:
• In worship settings where there is an interpreter present, or you receive the interpretation, and there is an orderly way to express God's message	
• Healing prayer team	
• Prayer team	
• Prayer for individuals as God leads	
• Private prayer language	

Quotations from individuals with this gift:

LN: "With tongues, interpretation and healing, we seem to have more of an on/off switch approach to it --- like of course I would know if I have this strange gift. But with other gifts, like teaching or administration, we allow more room for having it strongly/less strongly, or growing into the gift through training and practice. So, with healing and interpretation, we need to help people see the small things that might indicate giftedness, and then help them grow. Tongues has always seemed in that on/off category to me, but I am starting to see examples of people who seem to be in a gray area in between…One gal has a funny sensation in her mouth but no words, and another gal had some similar 'symptom' and eventually was released in tongues. I know two people for whom their 'tongue' might be Spanish --- they've put effort into learning the language, but for one of them there is something different that happens when she prays in Spanish…Seems like there is a fair amount of variety in how some of these manifest."

LZ: "It is a prayer language, but also provides for words of wisdom and direction. I use it most often in praying for healing for others, but also use it when I am truly desperate and facing something that strips me of my ability to segment my mind into rational and feeling, so I let the Spirit pray for me. I have found it useful when seeking spiritual wisdom and as a touchstone for when I need to ground and center myself in the Lord. The best part of having this kind of prayer language is the surrender to the Spirit, the sense of trust developed as you yield over cognition and the rational self for something that is lovely and pure, but wholly other. I find the prayer language varies, depending on what is needed: spiritual warfare, seeking God's guidance and direction as supplemental to scripture and counsel, when someone needs healing or help, and to tap into the peace and grace offered by the Holy Spirit as our counselor and comforter."

If you think you have this gift, write your own quotation (a description of what this looks like in your life):

Having reviewed this gift in detail above, who else do you think exhibits this gift?

Jot down your reactions/reflections here:

TONGUES

INTERPRETATION OF TONGUES

Those with the gift of **Interpretation of Tongues** help the rest of the Body of Christ understand the message being spoken by those with the gift of Tongues. It may be a direct translation of a known language or an unlearned language, or a strong sense of the meaning of what has been spoken. This gift may also be given concurrently to someone with the gift of Tongues.	This is one of my gifts _____ I am unsure if I have this gift _____ This is not one of my gifts _____
Questions on the assessment that pertain to Interpretation of Tongues:	Review each question and jot down what comes to mind:
When someone speaks in Tongues, I am able to understand the message.	
I am able to provide the meaning of a message of Tongues to others present.	
If someone prays in Tongues, I get a feeling or vision or picture of what the message means.	
Some words that describe people with this gift:	Put a checkmark below if you feel the word describes you:
Responsive	
God-glorifying	
Spirit-led	
Obedient	
Discerning	
Clarifier	
Some possible ways to serve using this gift:	Check which ways to serve sound like a potential fit for you, or add to the list:
• Anytime there is speaking in Tongues in public, there should be an interpreter so that the message can be understood by those present	
• Prayer team	
• Healing prayer team	

A quote from someone with this gift:

LN: "Interpretation is not always a translation --- it can be a feeling of what the message is about, or a Scripture might come to mind, or there's something you know you should do. Basically, all the ways we hear from the Lord in prayer apply to interpretations --- pictures, bodily sensations, songs, etc."

If you think you have this gift, write your own quotation (a description of what this looks like in your life):

Having reviewed this gift in detail above, who else do you think exhibits this gift?

Jot down your reactions/reflections here:

INTERPRETATION OF TONGUES

DAY FOUR   BEING THE BODY OF CHRIST

What Part of the Body are You?

The eyes? ears? hands? feet? Or, maybe you are the heart, the liver, or the pancreas? Jot your thoughts here:

The Apostle Paul says in 1 Corinthians 12 that the church is the body of Christ, and we, individual believers, are members (or parts) of that body. Each part is essential--just as our eyes and our pancreas are essential to our lives--to the church's healthy functioning.

We have each been given unique spiritual gifts to equip us to live out our callings in, for, and through His church. What gifts have you been given? Does it feel like yours are less important? Each of us plays a crucial role. How can your gifts be used to glorify God and build up the church?

So, are you the eyes—the person who notices everything, who sees people? The ears—someone who listens intently, who hears…or the inner ear—do you bring balance to the Body? Are you the hands—the one who helps, builds, crafts, touches? The feet—the person who feels compelled to go, to do, to act? Maybe you are the heart—the pulsing energy, the compassionate empathizer, or the liver—the one who helps the church filter truth from lies or good from bad.

Understanding what gifts God has given you is part of the greater adventure of gaining clarity on God's call and believing He equips you to do what He has designed you to do. Valuing your gifts and the gifts of others equally is also God's intent.

Once you are familiar with your own gifts:

1. Use your gifts. Ask God to use you. Ask Him to show you where you are already using them and to open new doors for you to put them into practice. Ask Him to help you embrace the gifts He has seen fit to bestow upon you.

2. Recognize that sometimes your use of gifts necessarily develops over time. Of course, God can gift you in a moment and make you fully able, but often we see that He gives the special ability and we live into it in stages, often reflective of our growing dependence on Him. Seeking those times and places to put a gift into practice can help further mature the gift.

3. Finding a mentor, shepherd, or coach to help you explore and grow into your gift(s) can also be a useful practice.

Living Sacrifices and Humble Service

Read Romans 12:1-2.

Define "worship" as described in this passage:

Does that definition expand your view of worship?

In what way(s)?

Re-read Romans 12:3-8.

List at least three ways we are to live as the Body of Christ:

1.

2.

3.

To whom do we belong, according to this passage?

For the seven gifts mentioned in this passage, list below how Paul says these gifts are to be used.

Gift mentioned	How this gift is to be used
Prophesy	
Helps (Service)	
Teaching	
Exhortation (Encouragement)	
Giving	
Leadership	
Mercy	

TAKE A MOMENT NOW TO PRAY and jot down 3 things you are learning about gifts:

DAY FIVE DIVERSITY, UNITY, AND PEACE

1 Corinthians 12:1 says "Now about the gifts of the Spirit, brothers and sisters, I do not want you to be uninformed." How will you commit to not be "uninformed" about gifts?

Read 1 Corinthians 12:4-6 and paraphrase the passage here:

What is the main concept of these three verses?

Re-read 1 Corinthians 12:7-11.
From verse 7, what phrase does Paul use for "spiritual gift"?

Again, from verse 7, why are gifts given to individuals?

How many times is the Holy Spirit mentioned in these five verses? What pattern do you notice each time Paul mentions "Spirit"?

What do you learn about the distribution of gifts in verse 11?

Read 1 Corinthians 12:27-30.
Look up the dictionary definition for "unity" and write it here:

Look up the definition for "diversity" and write it here:

How are those two things kept in tension?

What is Paul's point here with all the questions?

Read Ephesians 4:3-6.

What is our role with regard to unity? (See v. 3)

How many times does Paul use the word "one" in these verses?

What is the point he's trying to make?

Where do you see unity and diversity as positives in your church experience?

As negatives?

In what ways can you be an agent for unity and peace in the Body?

We are the church. Not the building…not any structure…but we, as humans, called by God, are being built into God's house. The church is more organism than organization.

We are part of a team—that is intended to work as a team. Scripture shows how groups work effectively together in the examples of Moses and the seventy chosen leaders sharing the burden of difficult ministry (Exodus 18); in the talented and multi-gifted group called to build the Tabernacle (Exodus 35-40); in Daniel and his friends standing firm, unified in purpose, eyes fixed on God (Daniel 1-3); in Nehemiah and the returned exiles rebuilding the walls of Jerusalem, facing hostility together, each person doing his/her assigned portion to accomplished God's purposes, all of which renewed their faith (Book of Nehemiah).

Jesus and His disciples were a team who did life together, learning, growing, being transformed. The early church exhibited the Body as they lived together, enjoying fellowship, meals, prayer, miracles, resources, and joy, with the result that their numbers increased dramatically. We also see the examples of missionary teams—Barnabas and Paul; Paul, Silas, and Timothy; John-Mark, Paul, and Barnabas. Through these groups of God-inspired people, the world has been changed.

REVIEW THE PAST FIVE DAYS OF HOMEWORK:

- From the Scriptures you read and your responses to the related questions, select one key lesson you learned.
- From the personal reflection questions, select one thing you learned about yourself, your call, or God's equipping.
- Transfer these two lessons learned to the chart on page 164.

SMALL GROUP DISCUSSION GUIDE FOR WEEK THREE

your spiritual gifts and the Body of Christ

DAY ONE: UNDERSTANDING SPIRITUAL GIFTS

1. Have each person in the group share their top three gifts.
2. Are there ones that people found affirming? Surprising? Confusing?
3. Have each person share their lowest-scoring gift, and discuss how these lower scores show a need for others.
4. What might the giftedness of your group or your church tell you about current or future ministry opportunities? What gifts seem to be missing? Why do you think that is?

DAYS TWO AND THREE: GOING DEEPER

1. Discuss what people discovered in reviewing the gift definitions, descriptors, negatives, and possible serving opportunities.
2. Help one another think through any surprises or confusion.

DAY FOUR: BEING THE BODY OF CHRIST

1. Share what part of the body each person thinks they are. Discuss what that means as a part of the Body of Christ. (Reference the Romans 12:3-8 questions.)
2. Talk about any insights from the Romans 12:1-2 definition of worship.

DAY FIVE: DIVERSITY, UNITY AND PEACE

3. Discuss the key highlights from people's homework responses in the 1 Corinthians 12 and Ephesians 4 sections, paying particular attention to "unity" and "diversity" themes.
4. How can each person be an agent for unity and peace in the Body?

◀ VIDEO TEACHING

- What spoke loudest to you in this week's video teaching?

NOTES

VIDEO NOTES
love, unity, and the gifts of others

*"W4 Love, Unity, Gifts" Video and DVD Available at GodGiftsYou.com **Password:** GGYloveunitygifts

love, unity, and the gifts of others

*U*ltimately, the context of using our gifts is in love. Jesus said, "My command is this: Love each other as I have loved you…" (John 15:12). We will be known by our love shown to one another. Paul goes on to say that our freedom in Christ is not a license to do whatever we want, but really a deeper call to serve each other lovingly: "For you, dear friends, have been called to live in freedom--not freedom to satisfy your sinful nature, but freedom to serve one another in love. For the whole law can be summed up in this one command: 'Love your neighbor as yourself'" (Galatians 5:13-14 NLT). 1 Corinthians 12 and 14 are bookends for 1 Corinthians 13—the love chapter. Paul makes it very clear that gifts are to be used in love—or they have no value.

Jesus...Peter...John...James...Paul...the writer of Hebrews—all say love is central. In the Old and New Testaments, we are reminded of this in nearly 700 verses!

THIS WEEK'S STUDY GUIDES

Day One: Love
Day Two: Oneness
Days Three and Four: The Gifts of Others
Day Five: Unity and Service
Small Group Discussion Guide for Week Four

DAY ONE LOVE

Re-read 1 Peter 4:8-11.
For each of the three gifts or behaviors mentioned in this passage, Peter gives a qualifying phrase. Write those phrases in the chart below.

Gift/Behavior	Qualifying Phrase
Hospitality	
Speaking	
Serving	

What do you learn from these phrases about use of gifts?

In verse 8, Peter says "above all" we are to do what?

What does Peter mean by "because love covers over a multitude of sins"?

Paraphrase verse 10 here:

What does it mean to you in practical terms to be a steward of God's grace (a grace-giver) to others?

Underline "so that" in verse 11. Why, ultimately, are we exercising our gifts?

Love and Unity

What do each of the following passages say about our love for other believers?

Passage	Love for others
Romans 12:10 Be devoted to one another in love. Honor one another above yourselves.	
John 15:12, 16-17 My command is this: Love each other as I have loved you. You did not choose me, but I chose you and appointed you so that you might go and bear fruit—fruit that will last—and so that whatever you ask in my name the Father will give you. This is my command: Love each other.	
I John 4:7-8, 19 Dear friends, let us love one another, for love comes from God. Everyone who loves has been born of God and knows God. Whoever does not love does not know God, because God is love. We love because he first loved us.	

Who is the source of that love?

END TODAY IN PRAYER—specifically asking God to empower you to be a "faithful steward" of His grace.

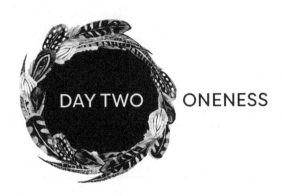

DAY TWO ONENESS

*Y*esterday's lesson was about love as the key to the exercise of our gifts. Today, we focus on unity and affirming other people's gifts.

What do the following passages say about unity among believers?

Passage	Unity
John 17:20-23 "My prayer is not for them alone. I pray also for those who will believe in me through their message, that all of them may be one, Father, just as you are in me and I am in you. May they also be in us so that the world may believe that you have sent me. I have given them the glory that you gave me, that they may be one as we are one—I in them and you in me—so that they may be brought to complete unity. Then the world will know that you sent me and have loved them even as you have loved me.	
Romans 15:5-7 May the God who gives endurance and encouragement give you the same attitude of mind toward each other that Christ Jesus had, so that with one mind and one voice you may glorify the God and Father of our Lord Jesus Christ. Accept one another, then, just as Christ accepted you, in order to bring praise to God.	
1 Corinthians 1:10 I appeal to you, brothers and sisters, in the name of our Lord Jesus Christ, that all of you agree with one another in what you say and that there be no divisions among you, but that you be perfectly united in mind and thought.	

Read Acts 2:42-47. In the NIV, this section of Acts is titled "The Fellowship of the Believers."

List at least 10 things you note about the life, togetherness, and benefits of being part of the early church:

1.

2.

3.

4.

5.

6.

7.

8.

9.

10.

Circle the one characteristic you find most attractive about the Acts 2 church.

DAYS THREE & FOUR THE GIFTS OF OTHERS

The Gifts of Others

Gifts can and should be recognizable within the Body. People ought to be able to see the gift of teaching or the generosity exhibited by giving or be convicted by the gift of prophecy. Take a moment now to see how easy it might be to identify someone's area(s) of giftedness:

Read Romans 16 where Paul lists some of his friends and co-workers. For many, he says one or two words that are a clue to their giftings.

Name	Gift or Role Mentioned	Benefit to Paul or the church (if mentioned)
Phoebe (v. 1-2)		
Priscilla and Aquila (v. 3-4)		
Mary (v. 6)		
Gaius (v. 23)		
Erastus (v. 23)		

As you may have noted, Phoebe's gifts may have been giving ("the benefactor of many people") and helps or leadership (deacon). Priscilla and Aquila hosted a house church—maybe that's leadership, possibly hospitality, potentially teaching or apostleship. Mary's hard work may indicate gifts of helps or administration. Gaius shows hospitality. Erastus' job as director of public works is mentioned, maybe a reflection of leadership or administration or knowledge.

In Acts 4, we see Joseph nicknamed Barnabas by the apostles—a name meaning "son of encouragement" (Acts 4:36)—likely because Barnabas had the gift of exhortation. In Acts 6, church needs were growing, but the apostles felt compelled to remain focused on prayer and teaching (part of their calling and gifting). So, they looked for people who were "known to be full of the Spirit and wisdom" (Acts 6:3-4). They chose seven, one of whom was Stephen, also described as "a man full of faith and of the Holy Spirit" (Acts 6:5-6) who additionally was able, through God's power, to perform "great wonders and signs among the people" (Acts 6:8). Based on this information, Stephen may have had gifts of wisdom, faith, and miraculous powers.

Can you identify one or more other Biblical characters' gifts? List those here:

Identifying the Gifts of Others

Refer to the Gifts Chart below, and complete the following:

1. Read the brief definitions and descriptors for each of the gifts.
2. As you do so, does God bring to mind a person or persons who have exhibited that gift? Write those names in the space provided on each page.
3. Pick at least one person and make time to affirm and encourage them and their use of their gift(s) this week.

Spiritual Gifts Chart

Gift	Brief Definition: Those with gifts of _____...:	Descriptors:	Name Someone You Think Has This Gift:
Administration	...bring efficiency and order to the church and to other organizations. These are usually the planners, goal-setters, or managers. They look for new ways to help people and tasks be more effective.	Organizer Strategizer Developer	
Apostleship	...introduce new ministries to the church. They blaze new trails, pioneer new endeavors, and step out into uncharted territory. They may have a great desire to reach out to unreached peoples and to spread the vision of the mission of the church.	Starter Entrepreneur Pioneer	
Artistic Expression	...have a special ability to communicate God's message through the fine arts, including drama, creative writing, music, and drawing. Through their God-given creativity, they use their gifts to draw others in and focus on God, His creation, and His message to us.	Expressive Innovative Creative	
Craftsmanship	...are uniquely skilled at working with raw materials, helping to create things that are used for ministry or that help meet tangible needs. They can be found fixing, remodeling, and sprucing up buildings, and/or creating and stitching items—honoring God and benefitting His people in practical ways.	Creative Skilled Resourceful	
Discernment	...distinguish between good and evil, truth and error, right and wrong. These people provide much-needed insight, point out inconsistencies in teaching God's Word, challenge deceitfulness in others, help sort out impure motives from pure ones, and identify spiritual warfare.	Intuitive Perceptive Sensitive	

Gift	Brief Definition: Those with gifts of _____...:	Descriptors:	Name Someone You Think Has This Gift:
Evangelism	...seem to be always seeking to build meaningful relationships with non-believers and are often able to steer conversations with these people to spiritual things. They communicate the good news of Jesus to unbelievers in such a way that they see people believe and commit to following Christ.	Forthright Influential Heart for the lost	
Exhortation	...offer a word of hope combined with a gentle push to action to those who are discouraged, tentative, or needing direction. People with this gift come alongside to offer reassurance and affirmation, and, when needed, to challenge or confront, all with the goal of seeing others grow to greater maturity in their faith.	Affirming Motivator Heartening	
Faith	...have that extra measure of confidence in God and His promises, helping inspire others to greater belief. Those with this gift live constantly in the knowledge that God works all things for their good and the good of others who are called according to His purposes.	Believing Hopeful Secure	
Giving	...have an extra measure of the ability to be generous. People with this gift live as if everything they have belongs to God, knowing that God will provide for their needs. Giving may involve money as well as other resources like housing, food, clothing, etc.	Resourceful Sacrificial Steward	
Helps	...meet the practical needs of others and of the church/organizations in order to enhance, support, or accomplish ministry. Indicators of someone with the gift of helps are that he/she serves willingly, cheerfully, humbly, and wherever needed.	Humble Available Dependable	
Hospitality	...have the divine ability to make people feel welcome and accepted--anywhere at any time. People with this gift enjoy connecting people with each other and creating an atmosphere where relationships and community can flourish.	Accepting Welcoming Friendly	

Gift	Brief Definition: Those with gifts of _____...:	Descriptors:	Name Someone You Think Has This Gift:
Intercession	...feel compelled by God to pray on a daily basis for others. They are completely convinced of the awesome power and necessity of prayer. They pray as a first response to any given situation, during that situation, and afterwards.	Faithful Trusting Aware	
Knowledge	...bring Biblical truth and God-given insight to the church. They may also receive a word from God that is uniquely timed and tailored for a given situation. People with the gift of knowledge may also be those who have a keen desire to study and know God's Word, and God may use this understanding of Scripture to speak a word of knowledge to a person or group.	Aware Perceptive Student of Scripture	
Leadership	...are visionary, good motivators, and effective directors–helping inspire others to achieve God's purpose. Leadership involves not only having a vision of the preferred future for the church or an organization, but also having clarity on next steps to achieve that vision, the ability to communicate vision in a way that inspires others, and the ability to equip the rest of the team to pursue the same direction together.	Visionary Goal-oriented Credible	
Mercy	...provide comfort, support, and presence to those who are suffering, in crisis, or otherwise hurting. Those with this gift reach out to others who are broken, having themselves experienced God in their own brokenness. They show God's heart to those who need the empathy of a listening ear.	Caring Compassionate Kind	
Prophecy	...have the gift that God uses to convict His people of sin and their need for repentance. Prophecy brings warning, challenge, correction, and confrontation without compromise.	Exposes Challenges Bold	
Shepherding	...provide nurture and guidance to others so that they grow in spiritual maturity and Christ-like character. People with the shepherding gift seek to walk alongside someone for a long or short season and direct them to Jesus and His offer of life, hope, and peace.	Fosters health Guide Counselor	

Gift	Brief Definition: Those with gifts of _____...:	Descriptors:	Name Someone You Think Has This Gift:
Teaching	...study, understand, explain, and apply Scripture's truths in such a way that people grow in their own understanding, are challenged, and are inspired to apply what they've learned. This can be done in a church or other context, since God's truth is true everywhere.	Communicator Inspiring Applies learning	
Wisdom	...use their God-given insight and information by applying it to specific situations, providing guidance in the church. They see the right course of action in the midst of otherwise confusing or overwhelming circumstances. Input from those with wisdom can shift a group's direction or help guide someone toward greater clarity.	Guide Perceptive Good judgment	
Healing	...follow the pattern we see in the life and ministry of Jesus where healing was physical, mental, emotional, and/or spiritual. Often also used by God to authenticate a message or a ministry. Always it is to show God's grace and mercy and power.	Restorer Responsive Intercessor	
Miraculous Powers	...help authenticate a ministry, encourage a body of believers, and show the power of God. In the life and ministry of Jesus, His miracles included feeding the multitudes, turning water into wine, raising the dead and walking on water.	Responsive Courageous Alert	
Tongues	...may speak in other languages as the Spirit enables them (Acts 2); may speak in an unknown language (that of "angels"-1 Cor. 13); may speak to God in tongues (1 Cor. 13). It can also be a way of "uttering the mysteries of the Spirit," and "sounding a clear call" to God's people (1 Cor. 14). Usually accompanied Interpretation of Tongues gift.	Responsive Expressive Worshipful	
Interpretation of Tongues	...help the rest of the Body of Christ understand the message being spoken by those with the gift of Tongues. May be given concurrently to someone with Tongues.	Responsive Obedient Discerning	

Who do you know who has been given gifts different from your own? How can you appreciate their differences and what they, by God's grace, bring to the table?

DAY FIVE   UNITY AND SERVICE

Today is about love and unity and service. We do not just see these commands to love one another in isolation. We see them in the context of every discussion of spiritual gifts.

Paul's longest treatise on spiritual gifts is 1 Corinthians 12-14. Right in the middle of those eighty-four verses is 1 Corinthians 13—The Love Chapter. We tend to use this quite familiar passage in weddings, but the context is gifts.

Love

Read 1 Corinthians 13:1-13.
List the gifts you see mentioned in the first three verses.

In these three verses, what value does Paul say these gifts have if done *without love* as the motivation?

In verses 4-8, Paul goes on to describe love. List at least 16 descriptors of love.
1.
2.
3.
4.
5.
6.
7.
8.
9.
10.
11.
12.
13.
14.
15.
16.

Go back and circle the one descriptor that comes most easily to you. Underline the one that is currently a struggle.

One great thing about stepping into obedience to Jesus' commands to love and to serve one another is that we are challenged—to forgive, to be humble, to go the extra mile, to put others first. When we act on our faith in practical ways, that engagement helps us see our greater need for Christ and the power of His Spirit to enable us to do the things He asks us to do. As we walk the path of servanthood, hopefully we are driven to our knees as our prayer life necessarily deepens and inevitably our worship is enlivened.

Read John 12:26.
What does Jesus call us, his followers?

Overlaying all this love is another important theme for the Body of Christ—we are the People of God.

Unity and Maturity

Read Ephesians 4:1-13.
List at least five actions Paul urges us to take in verses 1-3:
1.
2.
3.
4.
5.

How many times does Paul use the word "unity" in Ephesians 4:1-13?

What do you think "unity in the Spirit" and "unity of the faith" mean?

Read each of the following passages and note what they say about unity.

Passage	Unity
Psalm 133:1 How good and pleasant it is when God's people live together in unity!	
Ephesians 1:7-10 In him we have redemption through his blood, the forgiveness of sins, in accordance with the riches of God's grace that he lavished on us. With all wisdom and understanding, he made known to us the mystery of his will according to his good pleasure, which he purposed in Christ, to be put into effect when the times reach their fulfillment—to bring unity to all things in heaven and on earth under Christ.	
Philippians 4:2 I plead with Euodia and I plead with Syntyche to be of the same mind in the Lord.	

Passage	Unity
Colossians 3:12-14 Therefore, as God's chosen people, holy and dearly loved, clothe yourselves with compassion, kindness, humility, gentleness and patience. Bear with each other and forgive one another if any of you has a grievance against someone. Forgive as the Lord forgave you. And over all these virtues put on love, which binds them all together in perfect unity.	
Philippians 2:1-5 Therefore if you have any encouragement from being united with Christ, if any comfort from his love, if any common sharing in the Spirit, if any tenderness and compassion, then make my joy complete by being like-minded, having the same love, being one in spirit and of one mind. Do nothing out of selfish ambition or vain conceit. Rather, in humility value others above yourselves, not looking to your own interests but each of you to the interests of the others. In your relationships with one another, have the same mindset as Christ Jesus…	

It is clear that we are to find ways--with God's help, in his power--to live in unity with one another. Disunity does not represent who God is.

And, Scripture is also overwhelmingly direct about our faith, love, work, and service being deeply rooted in love—for God, for one another, for the world.

SPEND SOME TIME IN PRAYER—asking God to help you be an agent of love and unity in your church. Ask Him to unite the hearts and minds of those in your congregation so that the world around notices something profoundly and inexplicably attractive.

REVIEW THE PAST FIVE DAYS OF HOMEWORK:

- From the Scriptures you read and your responses to the related questions, select one key lesson you learned.
- From the personal reflection questions, select one thing you learned about yourself, your call, or God's equipping.
- Transfer these two lessons learned to the chart on page 164.

SMALL GROUP DISCUSSION GUIDE FOR WEEK FOUR

love, unity, and the gifts of others

DAY ONE: LOVE

1. Discuss the importance of love being foundational to our use of gifts.
2. Peter says we are stewards of God's grace. How does that terminology impact your view of service?

DAYS TWO: ONENESS

1. What do each of the following mean to you:
   - "Complete unity"
   - "Accept one another—just as Christ accepted you."
   - "No divisions among you."
2. What was most attractive to you about the church in Acts 2?

DAY THREE & FOUR: THE GIFTS OF OTHERS

1. Share stories of noticing, affirming, and encouraging the gifts of others.

DAY FIVE: UNITY AND SERVICE

1. What stood out to you from the Love Chapter (1 Corinthians 13:1-13)?
2. How does love relate to gifts and our use of them?
3. Ask each person to report what they most recall from the additional unity Scripture readings.

◄ VIDEO TEACHING

- What spoke loudest to you in this week's video teaching?

NOTES

VIDEO NOTES:
motivations and interests

Week Five

motivations and interests

Hopefully by now, you have already identified some things that shape God's calling upon your life. You have discovered your gifts and reflected on how those might be used in service. In addition to calling and gifts, your passions and motivations are important to identify. They help round out the picture of your uniqueness and point to places where and people to whom the Lord might be directing you.

As with the previous week's studies, you will look at important Biblical foundations and more concepts related to our universal call. Fundamentals like loving one another and living in unity are key to living as the people of God, the Body of Christ. These essentials can help prevent a healthy self-concept from becoming an unhealthy self-centeredness.

You are special to God and distinct from any other person who has ever lived. God desires that you seek Him first and live into His universal call to all believers as well as His specific call to you alone. May this week's study inspire and challenge you in new ways!

THIS WEEK'S STUDY GUIDES

DAY ONE: WHAT STIRS YOU?
DAY TWO: YOUR OWN UNIQUE STYLE
DAY THREE: YOUR STYLE CONTINUED
DAY FOUR: THE DARK SIDE
DAY FIVE: CONTEXT – LOVE ONE ANOTHER
SMALL GROUP DISCUSSION GUIDE FOR WEEK FIVE

DAY ONE   WHAT STIRS YOU?

The Bible is full of examples of unique individuals. No two are just alike. God has made you a certain way on purpose, with your own set of talents, abilities, gifts, and ways that you are inspired and motivated.

We cannot possibly care equally for every need we see or hear of in the world. Thus, God places in each of our hearts drives or desires or burdens that are those specific areas where we are more willing to make a commitment, get involved, even get our hands dirty. Those areas are what stirs us.

Sometimes identifying simple things like enjoying cooking or being a running enthusiast or working with children or liking travel reveals part of our hearts, our tendencies. On occasion, anger or dissatisfaction is a clue to where the Lord may want us to be an agent of change. Places and situations where you feel compelled to say "yes" are likely the places where God is nudging your heart—where you care most deeply. These inclinations may help us when we are confused about God's call.

Using the checklist of interest areas below, choose up to five with which you resonate most or add your own.

Sample List of Interest Areas

□ Accomplishment	□ Entertaining	□ Lay Ministry	□ Sewing
□ Administration	□ Environment	□ Leading People	□ Shepherding Others
□ Aesthetic	□ Facilitating	□ Learning	□ Showing God's Love
□ Animals	□ Facing Death - Any Age	□ Listening to People	□ Single Parents
□ Art	□ Families Struggling	□ Marginalized People	□ Small Groups
□ Authenticity	□ Family	□ Marriage	□ Social Action
□ Bible Study	□ Fellowship	□ Middle School	□ Spiritual Counseling
□ Books	□ Financial Planning	□ Missions	□ Technology
□ Camp/Retreat Centers	□ Friends	□ Mothers	□ Teenagers
□ Career Age People	□ Gardening	□ Music	□ The Lost
□ Career Women	□ Genealogy	□ Nurturing & Educating	□ Theatre
□ Children-Infants, PreK	□ Giving	□ Order	□ Travel
□ Children-Elementary	□ Goal Orientation	□ Organizing	□ University/College Ministry
□ Choir	□ (God's) Truth	□ Organizing Events	□ Unreached People
□ Communications	□ Greek System Ministry	□ Orphans	□ Women's Ministry
□ Community	□ Health Care	□ Our Church	□ Work and Faith
□ Computers	□ Helping People with Debt	□ Outsiders	□ Working with Hands
□ Cooking	□ Helping People	□ Parenting	□ Worship
□ Counseling	□ High School	□ People in Pain & Hurting	□ Writing
□ Couples Fellowship	□ Hiking	□ Photography	□ Young Adults
□ Craftsmanship	□ History	□ Planning for the Future	□ Young Mothers
□ Creativity	□ Homemaking	□ Poor/Poverty	□ Young Women
□ Crisis Pregnancies	□ Hospitality	□ Prayer	□ People Groups:
□ Cross-Cultural Ministry	□ Improving Things	□ Prison Ministry	□ University/College Ministry
□ Developmentally Disabled	□ Internationals	□ Problem-Solving	□ Causes/Issues:
□ Disadvantaged Children	□ Investing in People	□ Public Speaking	□
□ Discipleship	□ Justice	□ Quilting	□ Roles You Enjoy:
□ Education	□ Knowing God	□ Racial Reconciliation	□
□ Encouragement	□ Language	□ Seniors/60+ Ministry	□ Other:

Look at the 5 interest areas you checked. What do they show about where you are most willing to get involved?

Do you spot a theme? If so, what is it? If not, is there a theme to the role you play in each arena?

TAKE SOME TIME TO PRAY through all of Psalm 139—inserting your name into the verses. Sit with God, soaking in what He says about you and His creation of you, inside and out.

DAY TWO   YOUR OWN UNIQUE STYLE

$\mathcal{N}$ot only do we each march to a different drumbeat—what stirs us—we also have distinct preferences for how we interact with others and the world around us. There are many resources for discovering more about your style, your strengths, your personality type, etc. Much of it boils down to preferences.

Take a moment now to use the following questions to describe your own unique style:

Would your theme song be
- ☐ Working 9 to 5
- ☐ Celebration
- ☐ We Can Work It Out
- ☐ Do Not Stop Me Now

Or, would your life melody be
- ☐ Trust in You
- ☐ God is on the Move
- ☐ Put a Little Love in Your Heart
- ☐ Fear Not

Mark where you fall on each of the following:

Are you the

Strong, independent type   or   Collaborative, team-person

Do you love to

Be alone to get things done   or   Be with people

Are you more

Serious   or   Funny

Do you tend to be

Direct   or   Indirect

Are you more

Up-front   or   Behind-the-scenes

Are you more of a

Glass-half-empty person   or   Glass-half-full person

Do you

Love open-ended discussions   or   Would you rather cut the chit-chat

Are you more

Spontaneous/Impulsive   or   Systematic/Analytical

It is important to understand your own unique style, and to spend some time reflecting on how that distinctiveness influences your approach to life and ministry.

Some biblical illustrations of differing styles:
- The Apostle Paul can come across as intense and cerebral, maybe sometimes so forceful as to be offensive.
- Barnabas is known as faithful and personable, an encourager of others and a builder of bridges in relationships.
- Peter is viewed as strong, impulsive at times--an act-before-you-think kind of person, and a solid leader.
- James, the brother of Jesus, is the level-headed leader of the Jerusalem church, calmly guiding theological debate and organizational direction.

All different. All followers of Jesus. All likely with different sets of gifts. All with diverse areas of focus. Together accomplishing the work of God in the world. Together being more than any one of them could be alone. Each irreplaceable.

Are you more like:
- ☐ Paul?
- ☐ Barnabas?
- ☐ Peter?
- ☐ James?

More Scriptural examples of differences:
- Sarah seems to be a woman who takes matters into her own hands, is fiercely committed to family, and loyal no matter what.
- Deborah is powerful and influential, inspiring courage in others, speaking with wisdom and authority.
- Ruth is loving, kind, humble, hard-working, unselfish, and willing to be behind-the-scenes.
- Mary is faithful, accepting, and obedient, probably quiet and reserved, treasuring her thoughts in her heart instead of wearing them on her sleeve.
- Lydia is a successful businesswoman who is hospitable, persuasive, generous, and a seeker-after-truth.

To whom do you relate most when you read their stories?

- [ ] Sarah?
- [ ] Deborah?
- [ ] Ruth
- [ ] Mary?
- [ ] Lydia?

To whom else do you relate in Scripture? What traits of theirs seem especially like you or attractive to you?

Take a few minutes to journal about what these continuums and checklists have brought to mind about yourself.

DAY THREE   YOUR STYLE CONTINUED

How do you best connect with God?

☐ Outdoors?
or
☐ In?

☐ In worship with others?
or
☐ Alone?

Our preferences for interacting also extend to how we relate to God and His Word.

☐ Through Scripture?
or
☐ Through song?
or
☐ Through prayer?

Do you resonate more with the concept of

☐ Grace?
or
☐ Truth?

☐ Mercy?
or
☐ Justice?

Take some time now to identify a few more self-descriptors:

Are you more

| Adventurous | or | A careful decision maker |

Are you

| A big picture person | or | Detail-oriented |

Would you say you are (mark as many as apply):

☐ A risk-taker	☐ Creative	☐ Confident
☐ Adaptable	☐ Funny	☐ Generous
☐ Warm	☐ Helpful	☐ Friendly
☐ Thorough	☐ Practical	☐ Persuasive
☐ Impatient	☐ Insightful	☐ Compassionate
☐ Responsible	☐ Positive	☐ Uncompromising
☐ Organized	☐ Supportive	☐ Articulate
☐ Spontaneous	☐ Forceful	☐ Fair
☐ Efficient	☐ Intuitive	☐ Teachable
☐ Personable	☐ Candid	☐ Sensible
☐ Entrepreneurial	☐ Influential	☐ Imaginative
☐ Culturally-sensitive	☐ Humble	☐ Assertive

How else would you describe yourself?

How would others describe you?

You will have tendencies and preferences that are unlike those of others. How can you best use this diversity to pursue God's call on your life and use your gifts to the fullest?

The more self-aware you are, the better you will also know the places and ministries of best fit. Take a moment now to jot down your thoughts about your own tendencies and preferences and think further about how God is using them or might want to use them:

Where could these uniquenesses pose a problem for others who approach life differently from you?

Where might these provide an opportunity to rely on God?

Romans 12:18 says "If it is possible, as far as it depends on you, live at peace with everyone." How can you live into your distinctive character and style while at the same time seeking to "live at peace with everyone"?

REFLECT

- As you close today's lesson, turn to **Romans 12:9-18.**
- Meditate on these verses which tell how we are to live life together with others.

DAY FOUR   THE DARK SIDE

Whenever we explore the idea of calling, we can also struggle to embrace God's collective call on our lives.

You and I are called to be people who
- encourage one another and build each other up
- pray for one another
- love one another
- forgive grievances

But, at times, we instead
- criticize one another
- gossip about each other
- remain angry and unforgiving
- live in jealousy

At times, we may not want to hear God's specific call on our lives. Each of us is not just called to a particular Body of Christ (church) but also to our places of work or volunteering or neighborhood or family setting.

Where are you, in some of those places, saying, like Moses: Who am I to do this? I do not know enough nor have enough faith. I'm not good with public-speaking. Send someone, anyone, else.

Are you resistant, like Jonah, running from the call of God because you are afraid of what it might entail or cost you (Book of Jonah—see especially chapter 1)? Or, are you like Timothy, timid, afraid his youth will not earn him respect, needing strong exhortation from his mentor Paul to be able to fully step into his calling (1 Timothy 4; 2 Timothy 1-3)? Jot your thoughts here:

Let's take a lesson from God's responses to Moses (echoing the Week One study—Exodus 3-4). God says to Moses and to you and to me:
- I will be with you.
- I have an all-powerful Name that is rooted in eternity.
- I will give you gifts and abilities to do the things I have asked you to do.
- You may think you are ordinary, but I will use you to accomplish the extraordinary.
- I will be with you. I will tell you what to say and do.
- I am able.
- Go.

Are you in a place where you know at least part of God's call and promise but also have a strong sense that He has either asked you to wait or there seems to be some delay?

David was anointed as king and then had to wait and wait and wait, probably fifteen years, to become King of Judah and another five to become King of the nation of Israel.

Caleb was faithful but had to wander in the wilderness for forty years due to the faithlessness of others before he got his promised inheritance—a portion of the Promised Land—for which he still (at age 80) had to fight. (See Joshua 14.)

Where can you be "actively waiting," building spiritual muscle for the time in the future where God releases you fully into your calling?

Where can you be "faithful in a few things" before your Master entrusts you with being "in charge of many things"? (Matthew 25:21)

Or maybe you have come to depend too much on pastors and church staff. We act like staff are hired to "do" ministry. But God gives gifts to all believers, not a group of spiritually elite folks.

Perhaps you are waiting until you are a little more confident, a little more mature: "I do not know enough yet…I'm not ready yet." Just as there's no retirement plan outlined in Scripture, there's no indication that we're supposed to spend endless time on the sidelines instead of getting in the game. We see young and old, women and men, spiritual babes and the more mature, children and adults, with training and without training, all used of God.

We want certainty…but God wants our faith and our obedience.

Let's not overlook the additional fact that the enemy does not want this to work. If this is God's plan for the church, then sabotaging it is the evil one's strategy--trying to keep us wrapped up…tied up…dormant, unaware of our great worth. Satan whispers to us "you have no value…no one needs your contribution…just go to church, get what you need…and leave." So some of us leave these valuable gifts on the shelf. We buy into the lie that we have nothing to contribute, that we are not necessary to the functioning of the church. We live in fear—fear of risking, failing, getting out of our comfort zone--ultimately afraid to trust the God of promise and hope and power and transformation.

Read 1 Peter 5:8-11.
Detail Peter's warnings about the enemy:

What are we to do?

What will God do for us?

If you are struggling with the concept of call or your gifts assessment results, can you identify why?

- Is it something in your relationship with God?

- Is it timidity or fear?

- Is it an over-reliance on clergy?

- Are you waiting for certainty?

- Is the enemy whispering lies about your value?

- Are you comparing yourself with another?

We tend to think of gifting as being for the saints of Scripture or ministry "stars," but it is also for those who will never be famous. Exercising gifts does not have to look like Moses or Mother Teresa—it can look like helping get justice for a few people, or bringing one person to faith, or comforting one suffering person. Anything in God's hands is rendered significant!

Throw off the pressure to blend in or the tendency to be tentative. If anyone's gifts have gone idle/unused/underground for too long, then we have misunderstood how the church is to operate…and have settled for something *far less* than what God intended.

None of this process is about being obsessed with self, but seeking to follow faithfully while leaving the recognition up to God. Let God elevate you.

What is one thing you can do to remind yourself of your need to seek God in these things?

Additionally, where might you be tempted to view your gifts as either

- More important than others?

- Less important than others?

What is one way you can view yourself rightly?

SPEND SOME TIME IN PRAYER, claiming this paraphrase of God's word to Moses in Exodus 3-4 as God's word to you:

God says: I will be with you. I have an all-powerful name that is rooted in eternity.
I will give you gifts and abilities to do the things I have asked you to do.
You may think you are ordinary, but I will use you to accomplish the extraordinary.
I will be with you. I will tell you what to say and do. I am able. Go. Amen.

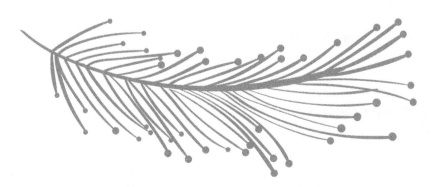

DAY FIVE   CONTEXT: LOVE ONE ANOTHER

Write out Deuteronomy 6:5:

Write out Leviticus 19:18:

Read Matthew 22:34-40.
What is Jesus' response to the question, "Teacher, which is the greatest commandment in the Law"?

The message of the Old and New Testaments is consistent—Love God; love others. Simple to say. Difficult to do.

Re-read John 13:1-17.
What is the setting/context for these instructions from Jesus to the disciples?

According to verse 1, what was Jesus' motivation for ministry?

How does He model that to His disciples in this instance?

In verses 14-17, what does He command them and us to do for each other?

What, exactly, does this look like in practical everyday 21st century terms?

Further down in this same passage, read John 13:33-35.
What is this new command Jesus gives the disciples and us?

What's the standard for this love?

What will be the outcome of us loving each other?

What's the measure of how people will know you are a follower of Jesus?

Where are you currently "busy for God" but perhaps less loving than you might be? How can you begin now to focus less on programs and projects and church involvements and more on how to love and care for those God brings into your life?

How can you see your whole life as under God's direction, authority, guidance, and grace?

Read Romans 13:8-10.
What debt does Paul describe in verse 8?

Sometimes Christians are criticized for their preponderance of "do not's." How would you describe how Paul puts it in these verses?

We've heard from the Old Testament, from Jesus, from Paul. Now Peter and John weigh in:

Read 1 Peter 1:22-23.
Write three ways Peter says we are to love one another:
1.
2.
3.

Read 1 John 3:16-24.
How do we know what love looks like?

List some ways we can love not just with our words but with "actions and in truth."

Reread verses 23 and 24. Love isn't just a suggestion, it is what: _____.

And we are empowered by Whom: _____?

Read 1 John 4:7-16.
Where does love come from?

Verse 12 says that our love for one another is proof of what?

Again, in verse 13, where does the power to love one another come from?

Rate yourself this week:

Not very loving   Love as Jesus did
    0   1   2   3   4   5   6   7   8   9   10

Take time to meditate on the **John 13** and the **1 John 4** passages.

SPEND SOME TIME IN PRAYER asking God to help you "know and rely on the love" God has for you, to show you ways to love in "actions and in truth," to love those around you deeply, from the heart, and to be an example of Christ's love to a desperate and lonely world.

REVIEW THE PAST FIVE DAYS OF HOMEWORK:

- From the Scriptures you read and your responses to the related questions, select one key lesson you learned.
- From the personal reflection questions, select one thing you learned about yourself, your call, or God's equipping.
- Transfer these two lessons learned to the chart on page 164.

SMALL GROUP DISCUSSION GUIDE FOR WEEK FIVE

motivations and interests

DAY ONE: WHAT STIRS YOU?

1. Discuss what people identified or discovered in thinking about their interest areas.
2. Have people share at least two things from this lesson about their passions or motivations, and how that impacts or might impact their approach to life/ministry.

DAYS TWO AND THREE: YOUR OWN UNIQUE STYLE

1. Discuss what people identified or discovered in thinking about their own unique style.
2. Have people share at least two things from this lesson about their style and preferences, and how that distinctiveness influences their approach to life/ministry.
3. Where do they see how their uniqueness might pose a problem for others who approach life differently? Where might these provide an opportunity to rely on God?

DAY FOUR: THE DARK SIDE

1. Where are you reluctant to embrace God's universal call or His specific call?
2. Where can you be "faithful in a few things" even if you do not yet have certainty about your calling?
3. What is one thing you can do to remind yourself of your need to seek God in these things?

DAY FIVE: CONTEXT-LOVE ONE ANOTHER

1. Spend time discussing the Greatest Commandment and Jesus' instructions to His disciples in John 13. What, exactly, does this look like in practical everyday 21st century terms?
2. Where are you currently "busy for God" but perhaps less loving than you might be? How can you be more loving and caring for those God brings into your life?
3. What do Peter (1 Peter 1:22-2) and John (1 John 3:16-24; 1 John 4:7-16) add to the "love" discussion?

◼◀ VIDEO TEACHING

* What spoke loudest to you in this week's video teaching?

Consider ending your time reading Psalm 139 aloud. Encourage the group to soak in what the Lord says about you and His creation of you—inside and out.

NOTES

Video Notes:
putting it all together

Week Six

putting it all together

When we think of God's instructions to His people (to us) we often think of the ones that begin with "do not." However, the ultimate command from God is to love—to love Him first and to love others next. It is a DO command. But, without Jesus and without His power, we are incapable of fully obeying that tall order. This week, we look at abiding—abiding in Jesus as our source of life and strength and power. Power to love others.

You will also have time in this final week to reflect on the previous weeks and continue to listen to God's voice through His Word. The study gets practical as you and your group explore real applications and ministry possibilities, while taking into account other important considerations like your current life situation and your walk with Christ.

Keep in mind that the idea is to seek God, learn what you can about your call, gifts, and interests, and try something. Obedience and service are not about guilt. They are about taking what you know about yourself and combining it with what you know about God and taking that one next step. It is about focusing not on the impact of your service but on Jesus, and letting Him direct the outcome.

THIS WEEK'S STUDY GUIDES

DAY ONE: ABIDING
DAY TWO: THE WHAT, HOW, AND WHERE OF SERVING
DAY THREE: MINISTRY POSSIBILITIES
DAY FOUR: OTHER IMPORTANT CONSIDERATIONS
DAY FIVE: ENCOURAGEMENT AND CHALLENGE
SMALL GROUP DISCUSSION GUIDE FOR WEEK SIX

DAY ONE   ABIDING

Read 1 Peter 2:1.
List at least five things Peter says we are to rid ourselves of in our relationships with one another:
1.
2.
3.
4.
5.

Malice…slander…envy. All rooted in comparison…in trying to climb just a little higher than the next guy. If you stop to think about it, envy is really anger at God—anger that God has given someone else something that I want or think I need. It is a way of saying to God, indirectly, "I'm unhappy with my lot. Why does he/she get/have _____(fill in the blank with your own discontent)"? When we seek to understand and live into using our gifts and calling in community, there's a temptation to compare. We need to stop viewing others as our competition, and instead view them as equal partners, equal members of Christ's Body. We're on the SAME side of things, not opposing sides!

Come to Him. Abide in Him.

Read John 15:1-18.
Who is the vine?

Who is the gardener?

Who is the branch?

What is necessary for a branch (you) to bear fruit (verses 4-7)?

What, according to verse 8, brings the Father glory?

What is one way you can remain (abide) in Jesus this week?

Constantly throughout the gospels—Jesus "called His disciples to Him"…to teach, to send out, etc. Our call, echoing this entire study, is the same: *TO Jesus first*…and then to learning and being sent and serving. You cannot go wrong if you cannot think of anything to do but to pursue (abide in) Jesus!

Read 1 Peter 2:10. (Remembering some concepts from Week One.)

What are we now?

What have we now received from God?

What is your response?

Read 1 Peter 2:11-12.

Abiding in Jesus, serving and loving others is life-giving. What do these verses say is soul-killing?

Instead, how are we to live?

What will be the outcome of living that way?

Read 2 Corinthians 5:14-21.

From verse 14, what "compels us"?

Whom do we now live for? (verse 15)

What ministry have we been given by God? (verse 18-19)

What are we called in verse 20?

Reflect here on what these verses mean to you in your current situation(s):

SPEND SOME TIME IN PRAYER—meditating on Jesus' words in John 15:1-18, seeking to "abide" in Him today.

DAY TWO · THE WHAT, HOW, AND WHERE OF SERVING

Recall the example of Moses you've studied in previous weeks. Moses likely had strong gifts of Leadership and Shepherding, and probably Wisdom or Discernment (all the people came to him as a judge). He may have had the gift of Intercession (always seeking God's face on behalf of the people). His call from God was to lead others to freedom. Put together, God used Moses to lead His people for 40 years from slavery to freedom... from Egypt to the Promised Land. God called Moses. God equipped Moses. Moses obeyed.

Maybe you aren't called to lead a whole nation across a desert wasteland…but maybe you and your Leadership or Shepherding gifts are meant to be used to lead someone from darkness to light…from a not-God existence to life with Jesus? Maybe you are being asked by God to use your Wisdom or Discernment to help guide your church or another person through an important decision. Or, maybe your gift of Intercession is essential to inviting the power and presence of God into a particular situation God keeps bringing to mind.

And, remember, an ultimate call like that of Moses often comes after times or even a lifetime of preparation, training, and faithfulness in the "smaller" things. Moses was trained in Pharaoh's household. Moses then became a shepherd in Midian. Moses was eighty years old when he began his ministry of God's call to lead the Hebrew people to freedom. And, there were many other "calls" within that last call: getting commandments from God for Israel, listening to God on behalf of the people, choosing leaders, guiding the building of the tabernacle, etc.

For you, it may be that you are in a time of essential preparation for something later. Perhaps God is asking for your faithfulness in doing one thing well before moving on to the next thing. Maybe He is training you now for a thing that only He can see off on the horizon of your life. Only He can connect those dots.

Jot your thoughts here:

Or think of Daniel's example. He probably had gifts of Administration, Leadership, and Faith. He also had gifts of Prophecy and maybe Knowledge. Add to that, God's nudge for the young Daniel to stand up for his rights and those of others and the later call to become a national leader of influence in a hostile environment.

Maybe you will not be taken into exile as a prisoner of war like Daniel, but maybe your gifts of Administration or Faith or Prophecy or Knowledge are exactly what God will use in your workplace or neighborhood or school or gym or book club or wherever God has placed you to live and speak for Him.

Jot your thoughts here:

John the Baptist's gifts looked like Teaching, Prophecy, and Exhortation. The call of God on his life was to humbly prepare the way for Jesus, the Messiah. Maybe you are to use your Exhortation or Prophecy or Teaching gifts to humbly prepare your church for something or urge someone to greater spiritual health.

Jot your thoughts here:

Businesswoman Lydia might have had the gifts of Hospitality, Helps, and Giving. As a result of her faith and gifts, she offers to host Paul, his companions, and ultimately a church in her home. Maybe you are called to use your gifts of Giving or Helps or Hospitality and respond to the nudge of the Holy Spirit to open your home for a godly purpose.

Jot your thoughts here:

Ruth's call was to follow the God of the Hebrews and be loyal to her mother-in-law—even to the point of moving to a foreign land, not knowing how she would be received and having no guarantees for her future. Ruth gained a new land, a new home, a new husband, and a family. She becomes the great grandmother of King David and is listed in the genealogy of Jesus.

Levi's call was away from tax-collecting, or at least away from the likely graft that came with that job, to following Jesus. Levi gained a new identity: disciple of Christ.

Rahab's call was away from prostitution and into a new forever-family of the Israelites and their God—ultimately becoming part of the lineage of the Messiah, something she could not have known when she turned away from her old life.

Are you called to simply be loyal to God and to your family? To move to an unknown place, where God has called your spouse or a family member? To leave a profession that consistently undermines your faith and creates temptations you are no longer able to resist and move toward a vocation where God directs? Are you being asked to turn fully toward God and away from your past?

Jot your thoughts here:

And remember, God uses everything—so do not ignore a talent you have or a life experience that makes you uniquely suited for something. It all counts.

Today:

Go back and review your notes from Week One. Write a summary of your lessons learned. What was most important that week? What stood out to you from Scripture and your reflections?

Go back and review your notes from Week Two. Write a summary of your lessons learned. What was most important that week? What stood out to you from Scripture and your reflections?

Go back and review your notes from Week Three. Write a summary of your lessons learned. What was most important that week? What stood out to you from Scripture and your reflections?

Go back and review your notes from Week Four. Write a summary of your lessons learned. What was most important that week? What stood out to you from Scripture and your reflections?

Go back and review your notes from Week Five. Write a summary of your lessons learned. What was most important that week? What stood out to you from Scripture and your reflections?

Do you see a theme? Something God seems to be saying to you? Write your thoughts here:

Your whole life is ministry. You are serving Jesus wherever you are, wherever you go, whatever you do. You have great significance—to God, to His people (the church), and to the world who needs to know Him.

Your call is one way God has appointed you to carry out His mission in the church and in the world. Your gifts are one way God has equipped you to do the same. This study and assessment may have helped you identify and further understand your call, your gifts, and those of others, but, ultimately, you need to get out and put them to use. The more you use your gifts, the more you will see new opportunities to use them. The more you exercise what God has given you, the more you will see as He sees and depend on Him for the fuel you need to carry on.

SPEND SOME TIME IN PRAYER, seeking God's guidance. If you resonate with a particular person's unique story in Scripture, go back and re-read it. See what God shows you in that moment.

DAY THREE MINISTRY POSSIBILITIES

If you are currently serving somewhere or see your vocation as a place of ministry, what do you love about it?

Take time now to jot down at least two other possible areas of ministry or themes that take into account your key lessons learned from the previous five weeks' study:

Spend at least fifteen minutes perusing online information, your church's offerings, or other local resources and make a list of possible places of involvement that you find of interest and possible "fit." Do not overlook ministry opportunities that may be right in front of you or may be informal (involving family, friends, your neighborhood, your workplace).

Location/Agency/Context	Serving Opportunity	Contact Information/Notes

If you are doing this study with a group, spend time letting each person share their list of possible ways to apply their gifts and call. Take a moment to brainstorm additional ideas for serving or focusing ministry based on how God has made them.

Jot down here the new ideas your group helped you come up with:

Location/Agency/Context	Serving Opportunity	Contact Information/Notes

Go back to both of the above lists and circle or highlight ONE place where you will commit to explore getting involved in the coming weeks.

In what ways are you feeling challenged about the discovery or use of your ministry gift(s)?

Every gift is not just for us to use. It is a reflection of the very nature—the very character--of God.

Take a few moments now to engage your mind and heart with the following Scriptures—maybe gaining needed perspective on your journey.

Read 1 Thessalonians 1:2-3.

List the three things that Paul remembers about the Thessalonians, then add the qualifiers:
(The first one is completed for you.)

We remember your...	Qualifiers
1. work	produced by faith
2.	
3.	

May your work always be rooted in faith in Jesus, your serving be motivated by the love of God, and may you endure because of the eternal hope you have in Christ.

Read 2 Thessalonians 1:11-12.

Paul is constantly praying for the churches. This might be an indicator of the gift of Intercession. **How** does he pray that God would empower them?

Why does he pray this? (Look for the "so that.")

Ultimately God deserves and should receive the glory.

Read Colossians 1:9-12 (in the NIV translation) and fill in the blanks below:

"For this reason, since the day we heard about you, we have not stopped praying for you. We continually ask _____ to _____ _____ with the _____ _____ _____ _____ through all the _____ and _____ that the _____ gives, **so that** you may live a life worthy of the Lord and please him in every way: _____ _____ in _____ _____ _____, growing in the knowledge of God, being _____ with _____ _____ according to his glorious might so that you may have _____ _____ and _____, and giving joyful thanks to the Father, who has _____ you [us] to share in the inheritance of his holy people in the kingdom of light."

Now, go back and **PRAY** Colossians 1:9-12 for yourself.

PRAY Colossians 1:9-12 again, this time for your church.

DAY FOUR OTHER IMPORTANT CONSIDERATIONS

Our involvements are not just impacted by call and gifting, but also by where God has placed us, our current life circumstances and responsibilities, our walk with Jesus, and our willingness. Spend some reflective time today assessing some of these categories in your life.

Current life season

Take stock of your current life situation. Are you in a transition (home, job, family, friendships, involvements)? Are you overly busy or bored with the things you are doing? Write a few thoughts about your current life season:

Where are you limited by real circumstances and where are you using circumstances as an excuse?

Walk with Christ

Where are you in your relationship with Jesus? Would you say it is growing, stagnant or somewhere in between? Are you feeling close to God or distant? Who moved? Sometimes our inability to clearly hear God's call is God asking us to wait. Sometimes that inability is rooted in our need to turn back to Jesus and away from other distractions that are keeping us from knowing Him deeply. Reflect here on your walk with Christ:

What is one thing that might help to make your relationship with God increasingly soul-filling and life-transforming?

Try something!

Still wondering what is next? Don't over-think this. Step out in faith and use what you know about yourself and what you know about God. Trust God. It is up to you. God does not seize control and make sure we use our gifts and respond to His call. We are given responsibility to use them. Learn as you experiment. And, remember where the power comes from! What's one thing you can try in the next month to experiment with your gifts and call?

Recognize that it is a process.

Find out more about gifts. Using your gifts and understanding them will take a lifetime. Growing into Christ-likeness takes a lifetime. Two indicators that what you are using is truly a gift:

1. It is your first response in any given situation.
2. Others can see it in action.

What is a common first response for you?

What do others note and commend about you/your ministry?

Learning what your gifts are NOT.

Do not give up right away if things do not work out exactly as you had hoped the first or even the second time. The experiences that teach you what your gifts are *not* are as valuable along the way as the affirming ones. What is clearly <u>not</u> your arena, based on past experiences?

Do not be motivated by guilt or paralyzed by comparison.

Ephesians 2:8-9 reminds us that our motivation to serve should be in response to God's lavish grace to us: "For it is by grace you have been saved, through faith—and this is not from yourselves, it is the gift of God— not by works, so that no one can boast."

And, serving in our gifts and call is not about being busier. It is about doing what God designed you to do. Be motivated by joy…by expectation…by curiosity of what God can do…by invitation.

1 Corinthians 12:7 (*The Message*) says, "Each person is given something to do that shows who God is. Everyone gets in on it." You do one thing. Someone else does another. No comparison needed.

And, in the end, it is not up to you!

Read 1 Corinthians 2:4-5.
Does Paul rest in his abilities or something else?

What is that something else?

Read 2 Corinthians 4:7.

What are we called in this passage?

To show what?

Read 2 Corinthians 12:9.

When you feel weak, what is the reassurance you have?

Read Ephesians 1:18-23.

Describe the power that we are promised in Christ.

Read Ephesians 3:16-21.   Underline the times you see references to power, Spirit, or love in this passage.

Now go back and **PRAY THIS PRAYER OUT LOUD**, claiming this for yourself.

We are promised God's power. God's all-surpassing power.
His incomparably great power—that strengthens, fills, enables us.
We can do far more than anything we can dream up ourselves—
because God's Spirit is working in and through us to accomplish
His work in this world.

Read Ephesians 6:10 (in the NIV) and fill in the missing words:

"Finally, be strong _____ _____ _____ and in _____ _____ _____."

DAY FIVE — ENCOURAGEMENT AND CHALLENGE

Through the completion of this study, you may have found affirmation that you are already in the right place doing the things that God has called/gifted you to do. Affirmation is a great thing! Your challenge will be to continue to see God where you are and always be open to Him making a change in your calling or how your gifts are used for His Kingdom.

Where has this study been affirming for you?

For others of you, this has been a great "aha" moment where you have gained clarity around God's call and are now seeking options for getting involved. At this point, a list of opportunities or brainstorming with others is useful.

What has been your "aha" moment?

For some of you, the study of gifts has helped you come to the realization that you are overly busy and too involved in too many things—maybe out of a sense of obligation rather than call. You may now feel you have permission to quit something. (This is the place where church leaders get nervous, but we really want people engaged where they sense God is gifting and moving, not because we have coerced them into engagement!)

Where may you be serving solely out of guilt or obligation?

Or, if you are still confused about who Jesus is and why calling and gifting is important to followers of Christ, you might seek out a place where you can ask your faith questions and come to know Jesus in a fresh, new, life-giving way. At the same time, seek some easy-entry serving opportunities where you can give of yourself while growing and being mentored.

Where can you learn more about Jesus in this season?

Take a moment to reflect on the messages in the following verses:

Read Daniel 9:18b-19.
Why does Daniel say we make requests of God?

What things does Daniel ask of God <u>before</u> he asks God to act?

On Waiting

Read Psalm 27:14.
Write it here:

Read Micah 7:7 and fill in the missing words and phrases:

"But as for me, I _____ _____ _____ for the Lord, I _____ for God _____ _____; my God will hear me."

What do these verses tell you about waiting?

Find reassurance in Jeremiah 33:3.
Write that verse here:

SPEND SOME TIME IN PRAYER about what you have learned.

God's vision for the church is that we be an appealing, exciting, alive, transformational force in this lost world…and He's chosen to carry out His vision by using an interdependent gifted community—us.

You will see things happen. You will give your gift to the church and the world and begin to see lives touched. You will look at your own life differently and see God at work in new ways. Serving as God desires transforms us. It alters how we experience God and how we view others. Service results in a renovation of our hearts and minds, and, hopefully, keeps us dependent on the source of power—God's Spirit in us. Serving as the Lord calls not only changes us; it changes the world, one act at a time.

From this day forth, may you commit to finding out how God has created your inmost being…and how he has shaped and gifted you to live and serve.

The impact of responding to God's call and equipping matters!
- Moses ultimately embraces his call and leads the Israelites to the Promised Land. (Exodus, Leviticus, Numbers, Deuteronomy)
- Miriam leads the Israelites in worship, song and dance. (Exodus 15)
- Bezalel does what he's designed to do as an artist, designer, craftsman, teacher—building the Tabernacle where God would dwell among His people. (Exodus 31, 35-38)
- Ruth, by her obedience and faith, receives a new family and a new heritage. Ruth ultimately is found in the lineage of Jesus. (Book of Ruth; Matthew 1)
- David becomes king. (2 Samuel 2, 5)
- Esther saves her people from annihilation. (Book of Esther)
- Daniel becomes the second most powerful leader in Babylon—after being a prisoner of war. (Book of Daniel)
- Nehemiah leads the rebuilding of the wall of Jerusalem in record time, also serving as governor of the province. (Book of Nehemiah)
- Mary gives birth to the Messiah. (Matthew 1, Luke 2)
- Paul reaches the Gentiles, and as a result, we are part of Jesus' forever kingdom today because of this legacy of faithfulness of generations who responded to God's call and used their gifts. (Letters of Paul)
- Phoebe serves as a leader and a financial supporter of ministry in the early church. (Romans 16)
- Priscilla and Aquila work side-by-side with Paul, not only continuing their profession as tentmakers, but also teaching, correcting Apollos' theology, and hosting a house church. (Acts 18, 1 Corinthians 16)
- Timothy overcomes his timidity, helping Paul plant churches, encouraging churches, and providing leadership and correction to the church in Ephesus. (1 Timothy 1, 1 Corinthians 4)

You have a lifetime to live this out. Consider the pace of a marathon and not a sprint. It is a long-obedience. A deep dependence.

You serve with your whole self:
- Interests
- Spiritual gifts
- Own unique way of relating to the world
- Current life season
- Walk with Jesus
- Abilities
- Profession
- Calling(s)

Read Colossians 3:23-24.
How are you to serve? List at least three things this passage says about work.

Whom, ultimately, are you serving?

Read Isaiah 65:14 and Luke 10:1, 17.
What common emotion is mentioned in Isaiah and Luke about those who serve?

In the end, we serve an audience of One—Jesus. Our service, besides adding value to the world in which we live, also brings us joy. As we give of ourselves (sacrifice), we offer ourselves in worship to the Living, Loving God. We offer grace to others, as we serve, being empowered, filled, and refilled by God's all-powerful Spirit so that we may "abound in every good work."

Remember **Philippians 1:3-6.** We can be confident that the Lord "who began a good work in you will carry it on to completion" as we step into obedience to His call on our lives.

Everyone who is reborn in Jesus has spiritual gifts as a result of that re-birth. EVERYONE. Let's be people who fully, eagerly, excitedly believe this truth. Let's unwrap and open the box of our gifts…and be unique.

Lest we also begin to think that we alone are doing these great things, take a moment to **read 1 Corinthians 3:3-10.** What are Apollos and Paul, according to this passage?

Who assigned them their jobs, their callings, their tasks?

Who causes the growth?

List at least three descriptions of us in verse 9:
1.

2.

3.

God's plan—to take a bunch of flawed people and put us together and make us His priesthood of all believers… to be ministers one to another—doesn't truly make much human sense. But it makes God-sense—especially if the impossibility of it is completely overcome by His power, His empowering of us, His indwelling Spirit, His guidance, His gifts. How much more attractive can our churches be if seekers can see that this something called church works by virtue of the power of Almighty God? May we act like we are "God's special possession" and faithfully "declare the praises of Him who **called you** out of darkness into his wonderful light." (1 Peter 2:9)

To those of you who volunteer in ministry in any church context, please *please* please see yourselves as God views you—gifted and equipped equal priests in the Body of Christ with significance to contribute. To those of you who are paid to do ministry at your church, please *please* please see yourselves as God views you—gifted and equipped equal ministers in the Body of Christ with significance to contribute. AND please *please* please view each other as equal and significant.

The hope is that you as a believer view your world, workplace, and neighborhood—the people with whom you have contact as ones to whom you can demonstrate God's love. It is about seeing all the existing opportunities right where you are…all around you. You are God's representative of grace and love and reconciliation—inside and outside the walls of your church. You are not simply looking for opportunities to reach others, but also expressing the unique ways that God has designed you. You are seeking to be a good steward of your gifts and abilities and experiences.

REFLECT

- **SPEND SOME TIME IN PRAYER ABOUT** the one or two things that stand out to you.

REVIEW THE PAST FIVE DAYS OF HOMEWORK:

- From the Scriptures you read and your responses to the related questions, select one key lesson you learned.
- From the personal reflection questions, select one thing you learned about yourself, your call, or God's equipping.
- Transfer these two lessons learned to the chart on page 164.

SMALL GROUP DISCUSSION GUIDE FOR WEEK SIX

putting it all together

DAY ONE: ABIDING

1. Discuss why comparison is such a temptation but also so toxic to life together.
2. What does abiding in Jesus mean? How can we abide in Jesus on a daily basis?
3. What does it mean to have been given the ministry of reconciliation?

DAY TWO: THE WHAT, HOW, AND WHERE OF SERVING

1. Where are you perhaps in a time of essential preparation or training for a future call? How can you be faithful in one thing right now without worrying about the next thing?
2. What is God calling you to right now? Did one of the stories in this day's lesson resonate with you more than another?

DAY THREE: MINISTRY POSSIBILITIES

1. If you are currently serving somewhere or see your vocation as a place of ministry, what do you love about it?
2. Have each person share their list of possible additional ways to apply their gifts and call. Take a moment to brainstorm additional ideas for serving or focusing ministry based on how God has made them.

DAY FOUR: OTHER IMPORTANT CONSIDERATIONS

1. After having taken stock of your current life situation, where are you limited by real circumstances and where are you using circumstances as an excuse?
2. What is one thing that might help to make your relationship with Jesus increasingly soul-filling and life-transforming?
3. What's one thing you can try in the next month to experiment with your gifts and call?
4. Discuss the power that we are promised and how this makes all the difference!

DAY FIVE: ENCOURAGEMENT AND CHALLENGE—MINISTERS OF GOD'S GRACE

1. Where has this study been affirming for you? or What has been your "aha" moment?
2. Where has this process been particularly challenging for you?
3. If God seems to have you in a holding pattern, how can you be actively waiting?
4. How helpful is the reminder that the Lord "who began a good work in you will carry it on to completion"?

◄ VIDEO TEACHING

• What spoke loudest to you in this week's video teaching?

PRAY Colossians 1:9-12 for your group/church.

Putting it all Together: Group Activity

Since this is a put-it-all-together lesson, pick one of these activities to do with your group:

Small Group Time:
- Meet as you usually do, spending the extra time in discussion, assisting each other with clarity and providing encouragement and accountability.

Gather Offsite:
- Plan an outside-of-meeting gathering at a cafe, restaurant or someone's home and discuss key learnings over a meal together.

Facebook Group Site
- Ask each person in your group to post his or her two key lessons learned and one thing he/she will do as a result of the study to a closed Facebook page created by the group or in a group email.
- Pray for one another's steps.

NOTES

A Summary Of Your Calling, Uniqueness, Gifts, Motivations, And Style

Week	Key Lessons Learned from Scripture	Key Lessons Learned about Yourself, Your Call, God's Equipping
Week 1		
Week 2		
Week 3		
Week 4		
Week 5		
Week 6		

Consider copying this page, tearing it out, scanning it into your laptop, or taking a photo with your phone—and keeping it in front of you where you can reflect on it, remember it, seek God's clarity, and put it into practice in the coming days, weeks, and months.

Appendix A

Note the Scripture passages that give some specifics either about the gift or about someone using this gift. You may want to go deeper by looking up and studying these chapters.

Administration

Scriptures that reference Administration or show someone exhibiting this gift:
Acts 6 (the apostles appoint the first deacons to help in the distribution of food); Genesis (Joseph); Exodus 18 (Jethro, Moses' father-in-law, instructs Moses in better organization and delegation); 1 Kings 18 (Obadiah palace administrator and devout believer); Daniel 2 (Shadrach, Meshach, Abednego--administrators over Babylon at Daniel's request), Daniel 6 (Daniel-one of three administrators over all of kingdom); 1 Corinthians 12 (in Paul's treatise on gifts).

Apostleship

Scriptures that reference Apostleship or show someone exhibiting this gift:
Ephesians 4 (included in the list of leadership gifts that are given to the church); Acts of the Apostles (throughout the book of Acts as you observe the apostles in ministry in a variety of settings and challenges); Romans 1; 1 Timothy 2 (Paul); 1 Corinthians 12 (in Paul's treatise on the importance and value of each of the gifts); Paul says that those gifts are given for the purpose of preparing others to serve in order for the church to be strong ("to prepare God's people for works of service, so that the body of Christ may be built up." Ephesians 4:11); Colossians 1 (Paul—an "apostle of Christ Jesus by the will of God"); 2 Peter 1 (Peter).

Artistic Expression

Scriptures that reference Artistic Expression or show someone exhibiting this gift:
Genesis 1-3; John 1:1-4 (God the Creator; Jesus—through Him all things were made; in Him was life; in Him all things were created); Exodus 15 (Miriam—"then Miriam the prophet, Aaron's sister, took a timbrel…and all the women followed her with timbrels and dancing; " "Miriam sang…"); 2 Samuel 6, Psalms of David (David and leaders—celebrated with all their might before the Lord, with castanets, harps, lyres, timbrels, sistrums, and cymbals; David—"dancing before the Lord with all his might;" "leaping;" "I will celebrate before the Lord"); Psalms; John 1; Colossians 1.

Craftsmanship

Scriptures that reference Craftsmanship or show someone exhibiting this gift:
Exodus 31, Exodus 35 (Bezalel and Oholiab); 1 Kings 7 (Huram—" Huram was filled with wisdom, with understanding and with knowledge to do all kinds of bronze work" for the temple Solomon built); 1 Chronicles 28 (lists priests, Levites, officials and people, but singles out "every willing person skilled in any craft" as a separate group to work on the temple); Nehemiah 3 (goldsmiths, perfume-makers); Mark 6 (Jesus—carpenter).

Discernment

Scriptures that reference Discernment or show someone exhibiting this gift:
Genesis 41 (Joseph—"discerning and wise"); 1 Kings 3 (Solomon—asks God for a discerning heart to govern God's "people and to distinguish between right and wrong"; God is pleased with his request and agrees to give him "discernment in administering justice" and a "wise and discerning heart"); 2 Chronicles 2 (Solomon described as "endowed with intelligence and discernment" given to him by God); Acts 5 (Peter knowing intent and dishonesty of Ananias and Sapphira); 1 Corinthians 12 (in Paul's treatise on gifts).

Evangelism

Scriptures that reference Evangelism or show someone exhibiting this gift:
Evangelism is listed as a spiritual gift in Ephesians 4—in the list of leadership gifts that are given to the church. Paul says that those gifts are given for the purpose of preparing others to serve in order for the church to be strong ("to prepare God's people for works of service, so that the body of Christ may be built up." Ephesians 4:11); John 1 (Philip brings Nathanael to Jesus; Nathanael believes); John 12 (Greeks seek out Philip to ask about Jesus); Acts 8 (Philip "proclaimed the Messiah" in Samaria); Acts 8 (Philip answers the Ethiopian eunuch's questions about Jesus; eunuch believes and is baptized by Philip); Acts 8 (Philip—people listened to him proclaim the message of Jesus and believe); Acts 21 (Philip "the evangelist" "one of the Seven"); 2 Timothy 4 (Paul encourages Timothy in doing "the work of an evangelist").

Exhortation

Scriptures that reference Exhortation or show someone exhibiting this gift:
Luke 3 (John the Baptist—"exhorted the people"); John 1 (Jesus renames Peter and exhorts him about his future); Acts 4 (Joseph was called Barnabas which meant "son of encouragement"); Acts 11; Acts 13 (Barnabas); Acts 13 (Paul); Roman 12 (included in the list of gifts); Colossians 4 (Tychicus was sent by Paul so that "he may encourage your hearts"); Hebrews 13 (writer tells the readers to "bear with my word of exhortation").

Faith

Scriptures that reference Faith or show someone exhibiting this gift:
Matthew 8 (Jesus remarks on the unusual faith of the centurion); Matthew 9 (two blind men-healed by Jesus according to their faith); Matthew 15 (the "great faith" of a Canaanite woman); Mark 2 (Jesus heals the paralytic based on the faith of his friends—"when Jesus saw their faith"); Romans 4 (Abraham—"against all hope, Abraham in hope believed;" "he did not waver in unbelief," "being fully persuaded that God had power to do what He had promised"); 1 Corinthians 12 (in Paul's list of gifts); 1 Corinthians 13 (in Paul's message about gifts without love—"faith that can move mountains"); Hebrews 11 (hall of faith—including Abel, Joseph, Moses' parents, Rahab, Samuel and the prophets—had "confidence in what we hope for and assurance about what we do not see").

Giving

Scriptures that reference Giving or show someone exhibiting this gift:
Luke 10 (the Good Samaritan—uses own resources to care for an injured person; also pays for the lodging and further care needed, without limit); Luke 19 (Zaccheus—after encounter with Jesus, commits to giving half of his possessions to the poor and repaying--fourfold--anything he had gotten through dishonest means); Luke 21 (widow gave out of her poverty "all she had"); Romans 12 (in list of gifts); Romans 16 (Phoebe—"the benefactor of many" including Paul); 1 Corinthians 13 ("if I give all I possess to the poor or give over my body to hardship"); 2 Corinthians 6 (Paul refers to himself and his co-workers as "poor yet making many rich, having nothing and yet possessing everything"); Hebrews 13 ("be content with what you have," keep yourselves "free from the love of money").

Healing and Miraculous Powers

Scriptures that reference Healing or Miraculous Powers or show someone exhibiting these gifts:
Exodus 15 (Moses throws wood into bitter water and the water miraculously becomes fit to drink); Matthew 16 (when the Pharisees demand a sign, Jesus called them "wicked"); Mark 2 (Jesus heals paralyzed man—it "amazed everyone"; showed Jesus has "authority on earth"); Mark 4 (Jesus calms the wind and the waves); Mark 10 (Jesus heals blind Bartimaeus; immediate healing); Luke 5 (full nets; healing of leper); Luke 10 (the 72 disciples sent by Jesus to heal the sick; demons submit to the 72 in Jesus' name); Luke 22 (Jesus heals a man's ear); John 2 (Jesus turns water into wine and the disciples believe in Him); Acts 2 (Peter speaks of Jesus—"accredited by God to you by miracles, wonders, and signs"); Acts 3 (Peter and John heal a lame man who walks "instantly" by faith in Jesus. "It is Jesus' name and the faith that comes through Him that has completely healed him as you can all see" and all came running to them); Acts 5 ("the apostles performed many signs and wonders among the people" including healing the sick and "those tormented by impure spirits" and "all were healed"); Acts 6; Acts 15 (signs and wonders done among the Gentiles through Barnabas and Paul); 1 Corinthians 12.

Helps

Scriptures that reference Helps or show someone exhibiting this gift:
Luke 10 (Martha making preparations to host Jesus in her home); Acts 6 (seven chosen to help with distribution of food to widows, to free the apostles to teach and pray); Romans 12 (service); 1 Corinthians 12; 1 Peter 4 ("serving").

Hospitality

Scriptures that reference Hospitality or show someone exhibiting this gift:
Genesis 18 (Abraham and Sarah offer hospitality to the three visitors); Leviticus 19, Deuteronomy 10 (love the foreigner, the stranger in your midst); Acts 16 (Lydia-invites Paul to home, hosts new church); Romans 16 (Gaius "whose hospitality [Paul] and the whole church here enjoy"); Hebrews 13 ("do not forget to show hospitality to strangers"); 1 Peter 4 ("offer hospitality to one another without grumbling").

Intercession

Scriptures that reference Intercession or show someone exhibiting this gift:
Psalms (David—Psalms are called the "prayers of David"); Luke 22 (Jesus intercedes for Peter—for faith, strength, not to fall into temptation, God's will be done); John 17 (Jesus intercedes for the disciples—protection, power, unity, truth, belief, love); Acts 8 (when Peter and John pray, the new believers receive the Holy Spirit); Ephesians 1; Philippians 1; 2 Timothy 1; Romans 8 (the Spirit intercedes for us "in accordance with the will of God"); Colossians 1 (Paul—I "have not stopped praying for you since the day we heard about you"; prayer for faith, love, power, hope, understanding, knowledge, wisdom, fruit, strength, endurance, and patience for them); Colossians 4 ("devote yourselves to prayer" for open doors for the gospel, for clarity); Colossians 4 (Epaphras "is always wrestling in prayer for you" to stand firm, be mature).

Interpretation of Tongues

Scriptures that reference Interpretation of Tongues or show someone exhibiting this gift:
1 Corinthians 12; 1 Corinthians 14 (necessary with Tongues so all understand the message; people with the gift of Tongues may pray for the interpretation).

Knowledge

Scriptures that reference Knowledge or show someone exhibiting this gift:
Exodus 31 and 35 (Bezalel and Oholiab—filled with knowledge and wisdom); 1 Kings 7 (Huram—made all the bronze items for the temple built by Solomon—"filled with understanding and with knowledge to do all kinds of bronze work"); Luke 22 (Jesus knows what the disciples will encounter when they go to prepare the Passover meal); John 1 (Jesus saw Nathanael before Nathanael came to Him and told Nathanael something true about himself); Acts 18 (Apollos was learned with a "thorough knowledge of the Scriptures"); 1 Corinthians 12; 1 Corinthians 13; 1 Corinthians 14.

Leadership

Scriptures that reference Leadership or show someone exhibiting this gift:
Exodus (Moses); Exodus 18 (capable men chosen by Moses and made leaders of the people); Numbers 27 (Joshua-"in whom is the spirit of leadership"); Deuteronomy 1; 1 Samuel 7 (Samuel--leader of Israel--"all the days of his life"); 2 Samuel 7 (God appoints); 1 Chronicles 12 ("the Spirit came on Amasai"--David made him a leader); Nehemiah; Daniel; Mark 10 (Jesus says the great will serve and the first will be slave of all, will give lives); Luke 5 (Jesus leads the disciples—who leave everything to follow Him); Luke 22 (Jesus—"I am among you as one who serves"); John 1 (Jesus—"Follow me"); Acts (James—leader of the church in Jerusalem); Acts 15 (Judas Barsabbas and Silas were "leaders among the believers"); Romans 12; Hebrews 13 (leaders—instill confidence, keep watch over as "those who must give an account").

Mercy

Scriptures that reference Mercy or show someone exhibiting this gift:
Nehemiah 9, Isaiah 55, Daniel 9, Amos 5, Micah 7, Luke 1 (God, delights to show mercy, the tender mercy of God); Matthew 5 ("blessed are the merciful"); Matthew 9 and 20 (Jesus shows mercy--heals two blind men); Matthew 15 (Jesus has mercy on Canaanite woman and her daughter); Mark 5; Luke 18 (Jesus); Mark 10 (Jesus has mercy on blind Bartimaeus); Luke 10 (Good Samaritan—took pity; bandaged wounds, gave transportation, took care of all night, paid expenses, "had mercy on him" where others did not); Romans 12; Hebrews 13 ("remember those in prison as if you were together with them in prison, and those who are mistreated as if you yourselves were suffering").

Prophecy

Scriptures that reference Prophecy or show someone exhibiting this gift:
Exodus 15 (Miriam); 1 and 2 Samuel (Samuel); 2 Samuel (the prophet Nathan rebukes King David for ordering the murder of Uriah and taking Bathsheba as his own; prophesies long-term consequences of David's sin); 2 Kings 22 (Huldah—predicts disaster, God's anger, reassurance); Joel ("sons and daughters will prophesy"); Amos 5 (Israel rebuked for injustice); Acts 2 (David prophesied of Jesus—he "saw what was to come"); Acts 11 (Agabus--predicted a severe famine); Acts 13 (Barnabas, Simeon, Lucius, Manaen, Saul; also mentions false prophets);

Prophecy Continued...

Acts 15 (Judas Barsabbas, Silas); Acts 21 (Philip's four daughters prophesied); all Old Testament prophets, including Isaiah, Jeremiah, Jonah, Micah, Obadiah, Joel, Ezekiel, Elijah, Elisha, Habakkuk; Acts 27 (Paul—predicts ship will be destroyed but all on board would live—"I have faith in God that it will happen just as he told me."); 1 Corinthians 12; 1 Corinthians 13; 1 Corinthians 14 ("speaks to people for their strengthening," encouraging, comfort, edifies the church; convicts of sin; "lays secrets of hearts bare," "message should be weighed by others," instructs); Ephesians 4; 2 Peter 1 (Peter—"I know…because Jesus made it clear to me;" "We also have the prophetic message as something completely reliable, and you will do well to pay attention to it, as to a light shining in a dark place, until the day dawns and the morning star rises in your hearts."); 2 Peter 1 (prophecy is not in human will or strength or understanding but "spoken from God as carried along by the Holy Spirit")

Shepherding

Scriptures that reference Shepherding or show someone exhibiting this gift:
Exodus (Moses); Psalm 78 (David--shepherded his people with "integrity of heart" and "skillful hands"): John 10 (Jesus—the Good Shepherd; calls by name, leads, goes ahead of, sheep follow, find pasture, life to the full, protective, lays down life for); Jeremiah 3 (God promises to give his people "shepherds" after His own heart who will lead "with knowledge and understanding"); Ezekiel 34, 37; Acts 18 (Priscilla and Aquilla to Apollos—invited him to their home and "explained to him the way of God more adequately," to further prepare him for ministry); Ephesians 4; 1 Peter 5 (Jesus; elders—watch over the flock, willing, eager to serve, "not lording it over those entrusted to," be an example, humble).

Teaching

Scriptures that reference Teaching or show someone exhibiting this gift:
Exodus 35 (Bezalel and Oholiab—"ability to teach others"); Gospels—Jesus; Mark 2; Mark 4; John 17 (Jesus—"I have given them your word…and they accepted it"); Acts 5 (the apostles "never stopped teaching"); Acts 11 (Barnabas, Saul); Acts 13 ("prophets and teachers," Barnabas, Simeon, Lucius, Manaen, Saul; Acts 18 (Apollos); Acts 18; Romans 1 (Paul--persuading, preaching, testifying); 1 Corinthians 12; 1 Corinthians 14 ("word of instruction"); Ephesians 4; Colossians 1 (to "present everyone fully mature in Christ"); 1 Timothy 2; 2 Timothy 2 ("entrust to reliable people who will also be qualified to teach others," "correctly handle the word of truth," "lead in the knowledge of truth"); James 3 (not many should be teachers because they will be judged more strictly); 1 Peter 4 ("speaks the very words of God").

Tongues

Scriptures that reference Tongues or show someone exhibiting this gift:
Acts 2 (Pentecost: all were filled with the Holy Spirit and "began to speak in other tongues as the Spirit enabled them" and visitors—each one—heard their own language being spoken "declaring the wonders of God"; actual languages of the nations); 1 Corinthians 12, 1 Corinthians 13 ("If I speak in the tongues of men or angels…"); 1 Corinthians 14 ("does not speak to people but to God"; if no one understands, need one with the gift of Interpretation of Tongues; tongues "utter the mysteries of the Spirit"; meant to "sound a clear call" to God's people); 1 Corinthians 14 (Paul says he has this gift).

Wisdom

Scriptures that reference Wisdom or show someone exhibiting this gift:
Genesis 41 (Joseph); Exodus 16 (Jethro, Moses); Exodus 31, 35 (Bezalel and Oholiab); 1 Kings 3 (Solomon); 1 Kings 7 (Huram—"filled with wisdom");); 2 Chronicles 2, Acts 6 (Stephen—"full of the Spirit and wisdom," the leaders "could not stand up against the wisdom the Spirit gave him as he spoke"); 1 Corinthians 12; Colossians 1 (Paul—"teaching everyone with all wisdom"); James 3 (wisdom which comes from heaven is pure, peace-loving, considerate, submissive, full of mercy, impartial, sincere, full of good fruit, humble).

Appendix B
Leader's Guide

God bless you for stepping into the position of leader of a small or larger group for this study. Here are some suggestions as you use this material:

- Pray before you do any planning, inviting, preparation.
- Be prepared with enough materials in advance so each person has his/her own book.
- Invite people to participate. Be clear on timing, expectations (for attendance, homework completion, participation, etc.).
- Pick a time and place of convenience for most in the group.
- Consider providing refreshments for your first meeting. Ask others in the group to take turns providing refreshments for each future meeting.
- During your first meeting, discuss group norms or commitments together as a group.
- Come prepared to lead the group—mostly as a discussion facilitator. Do all of the homework. Do any additional research you find helpful.. Biblegateway.com is a great resource as is Strong's Concordance online available through Biblehub.com.
- Do not send the message that you are the "answer-person." Allow for the group to learn from one another.
- Use the Small Group Discussion Guides provided at the end of each week's lessons to help you either in your preparation or your facilitation.
- Facilitate everyone's involvement. For quieter people, ask them to share their response(s) to a particular question or to read a passage aloud to gain their input. For those who seem to want to answer everything or talk a lot, encourage them to wait until others have shared. (You may also need to take these folks aside for this conversation if it becomes a problem in the group.)
- Open in prayer.
- Close in prayer.
- Rotate who prays, if people are comfortable doing so.
- Keep the conversation focused on Scripture and on Jesus. Rein in tangents, especially those that do not materially contribute to the subject.
- Follow-up with each person in the group one-on-one sometime during the six-week study to see how they are doing and where they might be confused or struggling.
- Consider co-leading the study so you do not feel like you are going it alone.

Appendix C
How to implement this discovery process at your church

1. Create a prayer team that will begin praying for the discovery process and planning efforts. Invite people to pray who are passionate about equipping and seeing everyone engaged in meaningful relationships and service in your church and the surrounding community.

2. Invite key people to be on your Equipping Ministry Team or Discovery Team. These are people who also see the importance of having this intentional process, ones who are willing to do the collaborating, creating and implementing, and those who have influence in vital areas in your church community.

3. Gain support from primary leadership—pastors, department heads, other staff, session, board(s), key influencers.

4. As you think this through, see if your focus is simply "plugging people in" or about "growing disciples more effectively"? Is there a culture in the organization that is about filling slots? Or a culture that focuses on helping people understand and live into the high calling described in 1 Peter 2:9: YOU are a "royal priesthood"?

5. Consider a two-pronged approach: one that focuses on equipping the congregation for meaningful involvement and one that focuses on pastors, staff, and ministry leaders to encourage them to adopt the same equipping mindset and make room for others in ministry. (Ephesians 4:11-13)

6. Be clear on your vision and mission. (See sample in this appendix.) Also take time, with your team, to articulate key concepts, set specific equipping ministry goals, and develop a realistic, but challenging, action plan.

7. Create job descriptions for all ministry opportunities at your church (and in the community). Many of these likely exist. Gather them together. See what's missing and fill in the gaps. Get ministry leaders to help with this. Help them understand the importance of inviting specific people to detailed job descriptions. The entire process improves from start to finish once these are in place.

8. Offer the *God. Gifts. You.* course as a six-week series at a time that will attract at least ten people to your first class.

9. Encourage participation in the class and the calling/gifts discovery process—so people can discover and/or further clarify their God-given giftedness for ministry and to learn the language of the Body of Christ. As you do, gather gifts, interest, ability, experience information from each person and develop a database. In addition, provide coaching to individuals seeking to connect. Eventually, you will likely want to have a discovery teaching and organizing team and a coaching team—but, early on, people on your vision team may need to fill these positions until you find additional members.

10. From your gathered job descriptions, connect people in your *God. Gifts. You.* classes to the positions that are the best fit for them in terms of their calling and gifts. Note: Their place of best fit may be outside the walls of your church.

11. Ensure that every invitation to ministry is grounded in a job description, an intentional, personal invitation, and promised follow-up.

12. Interview everyone who is invited and interested. Listen. Be sure that they know the expectations and support provided. Listen for a match between their interests, gifts, and life experience. Prayerfully decide. Remember, desperation never served anyone. Better to leave a position unfilled for a time than push someone into something that's not a fit.

13. Do your necessary screening and risk-management. Background checks, references, etc. should be mandatory in some serving contexts. Remember to protect your most vulnerable populations and your volunteers.

14. Once someone is invited to serve and accepts, orientation and training are essential. Have an orientation and training plan in place or see that each ministry has such a plan.

15. Determine what sort of ongoing communication, continuing education, evaluation, and recognition are needed. Make a plan for those. One of the principal reasons people leave their volunteer positions is that they feel unappreciated and unrecognized.[5]

16. The goal is to do all of the above well so that you retain these people as equal and growing-in-Christ ministry partners for the long-term.

On the following pages of Appendix C, you will find these additional resources:

- Mission, vision and general information for an equipping ministry effort.
- Hints for getting people connected in service.

EquipConnectServe Ministries
"equipping and connecting people for service"

ECS MISSION:
To foster a culture where all those at our church understand and live out their unique giftedness for ministry, and to assist and encourage them in finding meaningful places of service.

VISION:
ECS strives to assist individuals in discovering God's roles for them and how he has uniquely equipped and enabled them to serve. We connect with the larger vision of seeing our whole church family grow into the image of Jesus Christ, understand their roles in the Body of Christ, glorify God, serve others in his name--as an act of worship, and grow spiritually through faithfulness in serving.

ECS KEY CONCEPTS:
- All members of the Body of Christ understand and live out their unique giftedness for ministry.
- All are invited into the adventure of finding meaningful places of service.
- All believers are called by God to live lives of service. All are ministers.
- All believers are given spiritual gifts by God, empowered by His Holy Spirit.
- Christ is the Head of the Body, the church.
- The role of staff is to equip and shepherd the congregation for service so all grow to maturity in Christ.
- We are meant to live as an interdependent body of believers.
- Our serving is meant to glorify God and strengthen the church.
- Service produces growth in the one serving. Serving helps us grow to maturity in Christ.
- We are called to be good stewards of our call, gifts, and abilities.
- Serving is an act of worship.
- Serving is a faithful, grateful response to a generous God.
- All understand and act on the concept of "priesthood of all believers" (1 Peter).
- Each person is enabled to discover, understand, and utilize their God-given spiritual gifts, interests, way of relating, calling, profession, talents, and life experiences in ministry.
- "Ministry" is what is done inside *and* outside the church walls.
- Effective utilization of volunteers is essential for us to be effective in the ministry God has called our church to do. This includes appropriate recruitment, training, guidance, supervision, encouragement, challenge, and appreciation.
- Service to the community is meaningful, useful, and authentic. It influences others for and attracts others to Jesus Christ.
- Ministry involvement and giving/stewardship are intimately connected.

MINISTRY LEADERS:

As a ministry leader, you have the privilege of inviting people into the adventure of living as Christ-followers in every corner of their lives. Helping people see their whole lives as ministry, not just what is done in the context of Sunday or church, is a great gift you can give as you disciple them and engage them in your ministry area in various ways. This involves:

- Inviting people to understand that all they do can be valued as working for God.
- Inviting people to find joy in servanthood.
- Inviting people to understand that their service is a form of worship.
- Inviting people to see that they are grace-givers.
- Inviting people into God's call to serve.
- Inviting people into the adventure of discovering and using how God has uniquely gifted them.
- Inviting people to be an integral part of the unique, diverse community that is the Body of Christ.

Getting People Connected

Find a place for **NEW people** in ministry, especially new members and visitors—those who are "eagerly leaning forward." Create ways to gather their name and interest information and then contact them and connect them as soon as possible.

Create a spiritual gifts discovery process at your church.

Create a **Hotlist of Ministry Opportunities** and ask each ministry area to provide "job listings." Encourage all ministries to always be thinking of where their ministry gaps are and what kind of person could help fill those gaps. Make sure these needs are on the Hotlist…and, when someone responds with interest, follow up with them a.s.a.p.

If your church offers places of connection/fellowship/learning (small groups, classes, mentoring, etc.) with an "open chair" policy, consider creating a **Hotlist of Fellowship/Learning Opportunities** to make it easier for people to find those places of connection.

Create and make use of a database. Ask people to provide information about their ministry interests, talents, gifts, etc. and create a church-wide database that can be used to find the right person for the right job!

Communicate needs and areas for people to serve. Use all methods of communication, knowing that repetition helps. Never sound desperate, and always let people know the benefits of getting involved. Use social media, your church's website, your church's phone app, bulletins, pulpit announcements, emails, texts, flyers, and face-to-face and phone communication.

Connect in meaningful ways with the community. Add information about local nonprofit agencies with current needs to your Hotlist of Ministry Opportunities. Create ongoing relationships with these agencies.

Provide one or more annual All-Church Days of Service—a great way to build community amongst your congregation and friends as well as to serve in tangible ways where there are needs. Start first with those outside agencies and organizations with whom you have a relationship.

Invite people to get involved based on **giftedness and passion for ministry**. Make sure that what you ask them to do is not only a "fit" but is also meaningful and appreciated by you.

About the Author

Shirley Giles Davis has been on staff at First Presbyterian Church, Boulder as Director of EquipConnectServe Ministries since 1999, connecting people with opportunities to serve and places of learning and fellowship. She believes that discovering and developing your gifts is vital to growth to maturity in Christ, and that service is a key component of spiritual development and community-building. She has taught spiritual gifts courses to over 3,000 participants, and has trained teams of teachers, consultants, elders, deacons, university students, high schoolers, and staff. Highlights of her time at FPC include coordinating the Annual Columbine Elementary All-Church Work Days (since 2005) and assisting FPC's Katrina Relief efforts (from 2005-2010).

Shirley is also a consultant/facilitator/writer/life-coach with more than 25 years of experience in each arena. She has expertise in non-profit, government, and business management, leadership, marketing, strategic planning, evaluation, and implementation. Shirley has worked with a diverse clientele, including large and small businesses, city and county governments, state and national organizations, and religious and secular institutions. As a former executive director overseeing relationships with 228 agency clients and thousands of individuals, she spearheaded management training and technical assistance to non-profit executives. Her extensive media background, working for both radio and television stations for more than 20 years, adds communications and public relations proficiency to all she does. Additional capacities she brings to the table include curriculum development, navigating change, community-building, conflict coaching, volunteer management, and fundraising.

Shirley is currently part of the faculty teams for the National Sheriffs' Institute (executive leadership development), the Equipping Institute (Group Publishing), the Leadership Seminar Series on Volunteer Management (designed for church leaders and agency executives), and Your Unique Design Classes. She is a published author on a variety of subjects. Shirley holds degrees from Stanford University and Boston University, and is a graduate of the IBM Community Executive Program/Excellence in Management program, the Common Ground Mediation Center Conflict Coaching Training, Stephen Ministry training, and Spiritual Direction training.

Shirley has been married to Rob, Professor of Chemical & Biological Engineering at the University of Colorado, since 1982. They have two adult daughters, Grace (an anthropologist/primatologist) and Allie (a civil engineer). They all love to travel, and have managed to visit six continents multiple times in the past 10 years.

To contact Shirley to do a spiritual gifts retreat for your church, please email her at sgdavisetc@comcast.net.

Endnotes

[1] Dictionary.com, definitions of call, calling.

[2] These name definitions come from *All the Women of the Bible* and *All the Men of the Bible*, as accessed on BibleGateway.com's resources.

[3] https://www.brainyquote.com/quotes/authors/m/michelangelo.html, Michaelangelo quotes.

[4] https://www.barna.com/research/survey-describes-the-spiritual-gifts-that-christians-say-they-have/, by The Barna Group Ltd., 2009.

[5] Don Simmons, Volunteer Management Expert, senior consultant with Creative Potential Consulting, adapted from a handout received at a Leadership Network Conference.

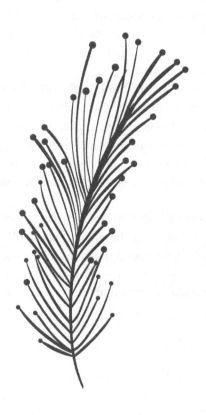

Made in the USA
Coppell, TX
04 June 2024

33118477R00098